POWER

THROUGH

TENSION

The Beauty of Unity

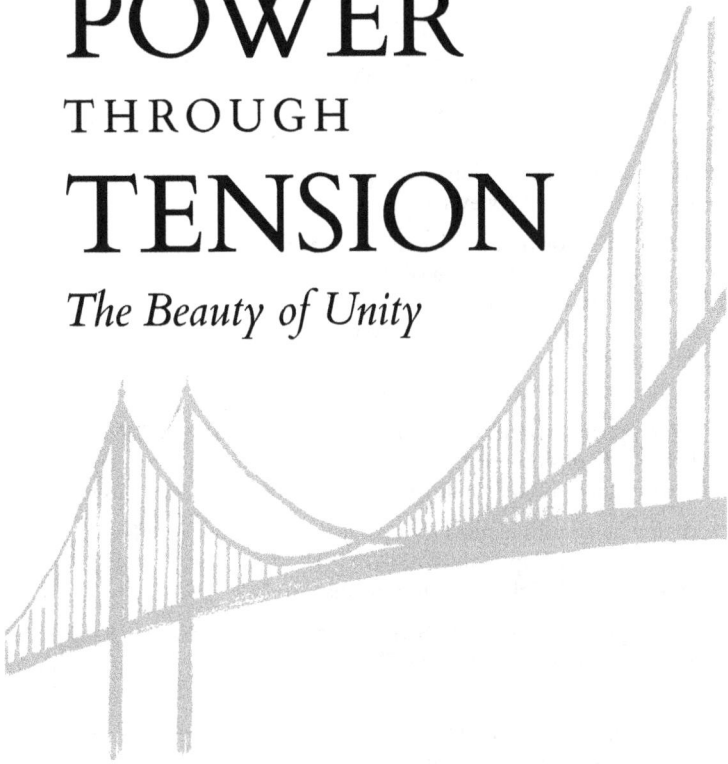

BRADLEY K. BETTIS

Endorsements

In the seven years that I have known Brad, I have seen his burning passion for unity for the church of Jesus Christ. He understands the cost and suffering that must be paid to achieve the great commission. Brad has aligned himself with the last prayer Jesus prayed on this earth in John 17 "that they may be one Father, even as We are one."

This young man has a burning passion to see God's church in its rightful place in the world. He understands Song of Solomon 6:4 that we will become a mighty bride as "majestic as an army with billowing banners." I believe this book will help achieve the admonition of Eph 4 "the unity of the spirit in the bond of peace."

Nick Lembo
Executive Director Street Grace AZ
Author of The Three Days

Power Through Tension - The Beauty of Unity is the most comprehensive and insightful book on unity I've ever read. Bradley Bettis delivers solutions for relational tension and keys for building bridges that are much needed in this time. I know we can all benefit from reading this important book, especially as we enter into election cycles!

Ann Tubbs
Co-founder of Transformation of the Nations

Power Through Tension - The Beauty of Unity echoes unity

from the caverns of Bradley's heart. The passion he has for the body of Christ is clearly evident. Each page is like turning and viewing a different facet of a diamond. You will see the power and beauty of running a kingdom race with a heart for reconciliation. Not as lookalikes, but as a unique and vital component of Christ's beautiful bride. The anointing that flows through unity not only transforms us, but also shows the world what true love looks like. Will you be remembered for your love of one another?

Ben Straup
Co-founder and Lead Pastor of Bethesda Church Northwest

Foreword

Bradley Bettis and I have "done life" alongside one another for 14 years. He calls me his spiritual dad, and as if he were my physical son, I learn as much from him as he may learn through me. We share life, talk nearly daily, take long walks, pray for one another and love deeply.

I have been and continue to be inspired by how Bradley lives and loves and pursues Jesus. He is bold and boldly in love with Jesus. He follows the prompts of Holy Spirit and starts and finishes the adventuresome projects God lays upon him. He wants Jesus to have his all.

I find his passion rich, unusual and inspiring. So will you. The same passion has him worshiping for hours, praying and weeping, executing building projects which become dynamic parables, and encouraging others. Within these pages, you'll meet him through the brief vignettes shared from his life and path. You'll also encounter his passion for God. And you will walk into the calling and hope granted us through the unity Jesus already purchased, which we get to embrace and walk in.

We live in "cancel culture," where disagreement means hate. People "block" and "unfriend" instead of talking. Everywhere we look, we find division and even violence. Families struggle to communicate across generational boundaries. Churches get divided by conflicts, but are afraid to admit it. We watch as whole denominations split over single issues. We need unity.

I spent 33 years pastoring local churches, encountering divisions, anger and hurt. I worked to help people learn and practice the challenging thing of actually talking across the aisle. I remember the Sunday two women brought their Facebook battle into church when they realized 'that was the woman' they were arguing with! What an exercise that was in helping people actually talk! Four years ago, I moved from the pastoral role to working with conflicted churches find reconciliation and peace through mediation and walking with individual clients in both mediation and counseling.

There's a deep need for healing and unity. Not unity meaning uniformity where everyone needs to agree or sign the same statement of beliefs to stay, but unity in the middle of disagreement. Unity of heart and spirit, around the person of Jesus, even while not agreeing about everything in life. My own children and I had to work for such unity during the COVID pandemic as we were divided by politics and viewpoints over the vaccine, but chose to love and stay in the conversation.

That's unity.

I am so impressed by what Bradley accomplished in these pages. He has written with such scriptural fluency and theological depth to grant foundation and breadth to the theme. God clearly has brought us to unity and called us into it.

My prayer for you is for you to capture God's heart for unity more than perhaps you had previously. May you experience God's own story and calling for unity to be expressed in new ways in your own life. And may this book be not just a read but a journey into a deeper walk. God has brought you here. I am certain. You'll be glad you picked this up. You won't walk away the same for having opened the cover.

So, what are you waiting for?

Brian Shimer

Mediator with Genesis Christian Mediation, United Methodist Church Pastor (Retired),
Author of Hello, My Name is Phillip

Dedication

To the Bride of Christ,

May we unite, becoming the powerful beauty embodied in Proverbs 31, who the forces of darkness fear and who Jesus delights in. Jesus eagerly anticipates returning to sweep us off our feet!

Acknowledgements

Jesus Christ: Thank you for trusting me with a message, giving me gifts, and loving me unconditionally. I am looking forward to Your forever reign, when Heaven comes fully to earth!

Bryna: Thank you for your support throughout this process, your encouragement, and your detailed eye that brought so much clarity. I love you, I am honored to be your husband, and I'm excited for our next chapter.

Mom: I loved your help with final edits, those interactions alone were reason enough to write this book - thank you, I love you! Also your six months of bedrest to ensure my safe birth astounds me; you are amazing!

Brian Shimer: Thank you for being the first to read the manuscript and for speaking life into me on this journey. Grateful for the years you've walked with me.

Meg Roberts: Your clear feedback and editing work shaped the main flow of the message. Thank you for creating a clear base for me to whittle into greater conciseness.

Austin and Amy Williams: Such precious friends. Amy, you nailed the cover design! Austin, our Marco Polos helped me flesh out ideas and to have a creative outlet to discuss brewing.

Andrew Simpson: Our authentic friendship started in fourth grade flag football! I deeply valued our Open Heavens 2023 road trip in the midst of this writing process, God has more in store!!

Nick and Jo Lembo: You are the answer to many years of praying. Mighty mentors and powerful prayer warriors, but most importantly beloved children of Jesus, I love you.

Eric, Christina, Jacob, and Faith Williams: Thank you for inviting me into your lives, for graciously helping me grow and mature in living out The Beauty of Unity and Power through Tension with you. I am honored to be in your lives and I love you.

Wednesday Intercessors: You are incredible! Thank you for believing in me, giving me a place to grow in leading, and going after Jesus to change the course of history - you are fire!

Bethesda Church NW: Thank you for creating a culture that encounters the presence of Jesus, prioritizes worship, and takes risks to unleash Heaven on Earth!

Imago Dei Community: Thank you for refining some of my rough edges.

Contents

Preface

In September 2021, the Lord prompted me to attend a writing conference at Bethel Church in Redding, California. I have written songs, creative pieces, and papers for my master's degree, but this stretched me, as the conference aimed to raise up authors to produce books. God met my obedience, faithfully pouring His presence over me in a tangible warmth and nearness throughout the weekend. I felt God calling me to write and then He started pulling a book from my heart. Like drinking from a firehose, I furiously put pen to paper, watching a book unfold.

When I returned home, I learned the disciplines of writing. Carving out times to write I made space, partnering with Holy Spirit, sometimes laboring to pull out what God had formed within. I've prayed for Holy Spirit to meet you as you read, that God would encounter you personally and reveal truth for your story.

I live in Portland, Oregon which has a reputation for being harsh and close-minded toward Christianity, especially Christian morals. Yet Portland is open and welcoming of various forms of non-Christian spirituality and lifestyles. It is also politically liberal. Frequently my beliefs and convictions are moderately to extremely opposite of the spirit and stance of the city. I write from this tension, believing this context actually strengthens the message.

The lens I am writing from is undeniably charismatic,

and I openly address the spiritual realm. I believe this material is accessible for a broad scope of readers, but I may guide you into unfamiliar language, ideas, and concepts, especially if you haven't had experience walking with Jesus in the supernatural. I believe by reading this you will be equipped with tools to engage in polarizing atmospheres, becoming agents of peace and hope for tense and divisive settings. I've written this book to Christians but it contains perspective and tools applicable to those not following Jesus. I believe that Jesus Christ is the Prince of Peace and the only way to lasting and eternal harmony. I pray for the love and power of Holy Spirit that changes environments, to flow in and through you, as you lean into tough conversations and yield the fruit of Holy Spirit.

If you are not a follower of Christ, I hope this book will lead you to Jesus. God loves you, Jesus willingly sacrificed His life for you. "For God so loved the world that he gave his one and only Son, that whoever believes in him shall not perish but have eternal life. For God did not send his Son into the world to condemn the world, but to save the world through him." (John 3:16-17). Jesus wants to bring fullness to your life through a relationship with God. Nothing else in this world can satisfy that deep longing. God has a spot for you in His Kingdom, He desires all people, tribes, and tongues to praise Him! May the love of God overwhelm you and may Holy Spirit bring you palpable peace.

The book is broken into sections.

- Preface & Introduction - Provides insight on my context and aim of the content.

- Section I - Addresses divides we experience, how to identify the source and move toward healing and unity.

- Section II - Provides ways of uniting that unlocks the power of synergy.

- Section III - How to leverage unity for dynamic impact.

- Conclusion - Ties the sections together with a brief recap.

- Appendix - Provides a historical example of the power of unity. This fits with the topic of the book but is supplemental material.

Introduction

Once, a friend came and helped me install cabinets in my kitchen. As we worked, we talked about life, reminisced, laughed and even shed a few tears. At one point we talked about those topics you have always been told to avoid: religion, politics, and finances. We had honest dialogue about differing perspectives and yet we honored our relationship through prioritizing understanding one another. We disagreed but created space to hear each other, express our differences, and share our process. We stayed connected and loved well. We asked questions, shared concerns, and stated hopes of our choices. We diffused contentious topics through creating space where nobody needed to be "right", instead opting to hear another perspective.

This level of connection is unity. Unity doesn't agree 100% on everything. Unity is more often marked by being for somebody and a willingness to work through areas of tension, misunderstanding, and difference because you accept and value each other. Protecting the value of one another is essential for unity. I can reject a person's political stance or perspective and still value the person. I can disagree about a religious perspective or interpretation and not hate. I can ask questions about financial matters, seeking clarity and insight, and not attack. I can love well and not fully understand how to handle something. There exists a holiness within tension. There is space to work together in the midst of not knowing what to do with something. We gain great freedom in asking questions and not having to live on the defensive. I don't have to devalue a person because of his stance on an issue. We need to cultivate valuing what God values. We need to cultivate caring for the people Jesus gave His life for.

The installation of my kitchen cabinets proved more fruitful than just new storage space. The task was much easier and faster with help, and included laughter and enjoying a meal together. We connected deeper through humility, listening, and assuming the best of each other. We added a chapter to our friendship. And now, when I'm in my kitchen, I often think of my friend. I believe God has many of these chapters for us. It is part of the fullness of God's vision for His united Bride. Our unity honors the beauty of our differences, yet submits to God's greater vision, allowing us to experience the fullness of His Kingdom.

The Apostle Paul encourages us to, "Make every effort to keep the unity of the Spirit through the bond of peace. There is one body and one Spirit, just as you were called to one hope when you were called" (Ephesians 4:3-4).

He writes of unity's purpose:

> *"So Christ himself gave the apostles, the prophets, the evangelists, the pastors and teachers, to equip his people for works of service, so that the body of Christ may be built up until we all reach unity in the faith and in the knowledge of the Son of God and become mature, attaining to the whole measure of the fullness of Christ. Then we will no longer be infants, tossed back and forth by the waves, and*

blown here and there by every wind of teaching
and by the cunning and craftiness of people in
their deceitful scheming. Instead, speaking the truth
in love, we will grow to become in every respect
the mature body of him who is the head, that is,
Christ. From him the whole body, joined and held
together by every supporting ligament, grows and
builds itself up in love, as each part does its work."
(Ephesians 4:11-16)

Paul describes a radical level of dependency, revealing that self-sufficiency is not the call of Jesus. We are not designed to function on our own. God wants beauty from relationships. Something greater through the interconnection of the body of Christ. This outshines the independent way of the Western mindset.

We live in a time where disconnect and distance reigns. It has become socially acceptable to speak your mind and elevate an issue or stance above a person. Even saying whatever is necessary to prove you are "right". This includes name calling, canceling, and judging that condemns others. When actions are purposefully harmful and divisive, we've partnered with the wrong kingdom.

Jesus modeled a love focused life. "Perfect love casts out fear" (1 John 4:18), and "Love covers over a multitude of sins" (1 Peter 4:8). As we follow Jesus, our target becomes loving each other, not proving others wrong. This doesn't mean we disregard standards and ignore the principles of the Kingdom of God. God has fixed values and healthy ways for His kids to follow. The tension exists that we live in different levels of maturity and sometimes we still get caught trying to prove others wrong, when we need to extend love. Our goal is to create space for people to experience Jesus and be transformed by encountering His love, not guilting people into behavior change. God provides margin and mercy for our process to reach this goal.

Jesus knows we need to mature. King Solomon aptly wrote, "as iron sharpens iron, so one person sharpens another." (Proverbs 27:17). We gain from embracing the tensions of relationships, especially with people very different from us. Sharpening makes us more effective, but this refining hurts. When we disagree, we do not have license to slander another, even if the position held is clearly misaligned. There is no slander in heaven. Slander is saying something false about a person, and as followers of Jesus we are called to speak the truth of Jesus' redemption over one another. To slander a believer of Jesus, even due to an atrocious sin, is to imply that Jesus' blood is insufficient. Elevating sinful behavior above the redemptive power of Jesus' sacrifice creates a divide. Heaven has no division.

Jesus sees you and me in the vileness of our sin–a true understanding that is way more brutal and awful than we can grasp–yet He extends mercy, grace, and compassion to us. He models what it looks like to interact with those you disagree with. If anyone had the right to reject, cancel, or destroy others, it would be Jesus. But instead, He redeems. He holds no wrong against us. He harbors no bitterness. He offers us the model of grace. He is the most wronged human in all of history. He experienced injustice at the maximum capacity. Everything plotted against Him was unfounded. Every burden He bore, beating He took, and the death He died were all violations of justice. These were sins against love, sins against truth, sins against perfection. The prophet Isaiah, foretold of Jesus, "He was oppressed and afflicted, yet he did not open his mouth; he was led like a lamb to the slaughter, and as a sheep before its shearers is silent, so he did not open his mouth." (Isaiah 53:7). He offered honor, grace, and love, even when He was wrongly mocked, scourged, and crucified. He never acted apart from these core values and necessary ways of loving and engaging His children. He modeled perfect humanity. This is only attainable through His blood and by His Spirit.

Jesus lived in times of disorder and division and showed the necessity of unity to experience the fullness of the Kingdom. For us to walk through our polarizing time, we need unity. We need to let go of a desire to shame and harm and lash out in retributive "justice", and instead extend love.

> "Love endures with patience and serenity, love is
> kind and thoughtful, and is not jealous or envious;
> love does not brag and is not proud or arrogant. It
> is not rude; it is not self-seeking, it is not provoked
> [nor overly sensitive and easily angered]; it does
> not take into account a wrong endured. It does not
> rejoice at injustice, but rejoices with the truth [when
> right and truth prevail]. Love bears all things
> [regardless of what comes], believes all things
> [looking for the best in each one], hopes all things
> [remaining steadfast during difficult times], endures
> all things [without weakening]. Love never fails
> (it never fades nor ends)." (1 Corinthians 13: 4-8
> AMP)

This is the DNA of unity that Jesus desires for us. I believe "nor overly sensitive and easily angered" is essential for our time. We cannot get caught in the spirit of the age that is raging, condemning, and finger pointing. We need a deeper connection with Holy Spirit so that we can respond with love that overwhelms condemnation. We also need to understand our emotions, identify the root causes of these explosive forces, and bring these to Jesus for understanding and healing. Proverbs 20:5 "The purposes of a man's heart are deep waters, but a man of understanding draws them out." Jesus has a deep understanding that helps us discover our purpose, and overcome barriers of it. He can reveal hurts and the source of emotional explosions that prevent us from achieving what He desires. As we bring our pains to Him we gain means to heal from pains embedded within. This leads us to active choices rather than reactive ones. These active choices include expressing love by holding our tongues when everything in us wants to say harmful things.

We gain much through connection and building collectively.

> "God has so composed the body, giving more
> abundant honor to that part which lacked, so that
> there may be no division in the body, but that
> the parts may have the same care for one another.
> And if one part of the body suffers, all the parts
> suffer with it; if a part is honored, all the parts
> rejoice with it. Now you are Christ's body, and
> individually parts of it." (1 Corinthians 12:24-27
> NASB)

Paul wrote this to a fragmented Corinthian church, where people were elevating themselves over each other, rather than serving to support the body. We need each other, we are designed to work collaboratively. We are one body. There are limits to what we can do on our own and incredible things we can do collectively.

This book calls us to journey toward wholeness. It is an invitation to look at ourselves, our pains, and our purpose to recognize we heal and flourish within the body of Christ, where we support the collective flourishing. We were designed to thrive together, accomplishing the work of Jesus, and destroying the kingdom of darkness through revealing Christ. Our ultimate call is to be one Bride for the Bridegroom of Heaven to love and enjoy. To come together, we have to look at the root of what is tearing us apart.

Define and Face Our Problem

CHAPTER 1

Origins of the Independent Mindset

For those of us in the West, especially the United States, we've been baptized in a culture of independence, especially post-World War II. Prior to the post-war boom, the social systems and structures had greater levels of consistency, tradition, even limitations, that were framed by strong levels of interdependence. These traditional ways created a stable society with great strength. Yet these ways often lacked the vision and creativity for exploratory ideas. The irony here is the United States is a nation founded on the principles of risk, breaking the mold, and pathfinding. From the Pilgrims who first settled across the Atlantic, then Lewis and Clark explored the great West. Pioneers followed with wagon trains, establishing settlements in these wild territories. In the DNA of the American is the will to do things differently, to envision, and trailblaze an alternative way.

Often, following on the heels of a trailblazing

generation is a settling generation that works to establish consistency and stability. This seems to be a largely cyclical pattern in human history. One generation launches, explores, and conquers, the next develops, establishes, and settles the wild into a well-stewarded system.

Arguably the generation that fought World War II was a settling generation and the post war generation was a pioneering generation. Prior to the war the patterns were largely consistent: men frequently followed in the professional footsteps of their fathers, women cared for the home and raised their children, and the vision of a healthy community took on a traditional mold. Outliers and pioneers can be found in any culture or time, but the era pre-1950 is quite a contrast to the postmodern era, marked by challenging absolutes and often rejecting the previously rooted ways of life.

My Nana is in her late eighties and she can share many stories about the simplicity and limitations of life she experienced before 1950, both as a child in the Midwest and young adult in the Pacific Northwest. For example, when she attended college she had only three options; she could train to be a secretary, nurse, or teacher. She chose to be a teacher.

At that time, family units were central to the everyday systems of life and roles existed that, by and large, were traditional with minimal variety. This included gender roles, socio-economic position, diet, employment, and location where one lived. There was a lot more long standing continuity and less movement. Changes happened but not at the pace or frequency of our time. Collective community mindset was the general norm and the world wars further catalyzed this, both through the destructive pain of loss of family members, as well as the willingness of people to sacrifice for the greater good of winning the war. Loss and hard times have the potential to unite people.

This was a time when independence was minimized and the free choices of an individual were limited to small personal preferences. The requirements of fighting the wars and the sacrificial effort to win led the charge. It seems the post-war boom, the ramping up of the economy, and the explosive population growth paved roads for difference. Again, this boom represented part, but not all, of God's heart. Great things came from advancement and from fanning the flames of uniqueness. However, in this time without the outside force of a worldwide fight against evil, many of the sacrificial and uniting actions were no longer prevalent or necessary. Freedoms emerged and differences began to flourish.

God desires to unite people, glorifying Himself through the various expressions, as stated in Isaiah 66:18, He wants "all nations and tongues, and they will come and see my glory." Throughout the Bible God values unique and varied expression, grafting in and uniting all who willingly submit to His Kingdom and ways. He made provision for non-Jews to participate in Passover (Exodus 12:48-49). He included Rahab, a non-Hebrew resident of Jericho in His plan that brought Israel into the Promised Land (Hebrews 11:31). David's list of mighty men in 1 Chronicles 11 includes Zelek the Ammonite (v39), Uriah the Hittite (v41), and Ithmah the Moabite (v46). Paul writes that Gentile believers have been grafted into the redemption that God provided first for the Jewish people.

"If some of the branches have been broken off, and you, though a wild olive shoot, have been grafted in

among the others and now share in the nourishing
sap from the olive root, do not consider yourself
to be superior to those other branches. If you do,
consider this: You do not support the root, but the
root supports you". (Romans 11:17-18)

God's Bride includes all people. He connects all our differences around the only thing we can unite on: experiencing the presence and glory of Jesus.

During the 1940s and beyond with explosive change and the celebration of difference, the concept of being self-made and independent grew. Self-sufficiency and independence have positive expressions, but in and of themselves, these concepts are antithetical to Jesus. He leads us to submit and live in connection with Him. As Jesus said in John 15:5, "I am the vine and you are the branches. If a man remains in me and I in him, he will bear much fruit; apart from me you can do nothing." This statement dismantles the idea that Jesus wants us to prove ourselves to Him. Jesus is referencing a grape vine and how we, the branches, extend from Him, the vine. Life and power flows from the vine. When severed from the vine, the branch has no means of producing fruit, let alone sustaining life. This "what you do with the gifts given to you, is your gift to God" theology partners with the ancient Greek mindset, an individualistic approach and with self-made expectations. Much of the Western mindset derives from this and is prone to isolation and siloing which plays right into the tactics of our enemy who, "prowls around like a roaring lion, looking for someone to devour" (1 Peter 5:8).

Though an appealing idea, it is not possible to produce fruit on our own that will cause God to take greater pleasure in us. We bear fruit through connection with Jesus, the

Vine, through submitting and humbly partnering with God in His ways and purposes. Proverbs 20:24 sheds light on this, "A man's steps are directed by the Lord. How then can anyone understand his own way?". We cannot cause ourselves to succeed and prosper apart from God. Our efforts to produce righteousness apart from God are worthless (Isaiah 64:6), so fame, fortune and achieving the world's definition of success apart from God yield no eternal value. Self-made independence is a tactic that our enemy employs to trap us, leading us into a death camp. He can and will use success and abundance to isolate so that he can devour your morality and eventually your spirit. God will always know things about us that will require a relationship with Him to understand. We can mine a great depth about who we are, but we will never thrive apart from the partnership with our Creator and Father who causes us to thrive. We simply will not thrive on our own.

Jesus designed us to be interdependent both with Him and with others. In fact our partnership and leaning into the various strengths of those around us allows Him to receive greater glory. He will still assign us independent tasks. But independence is never meant to validate who we are by offering something to God that we've done ourselves. As Isaiah 64:6 says, "all of our righteous acts are like filthy rags"; without God in our process we yield nothing worthwhile. The value comes from first receiving and being immersed in God's love, the overflow produces abundant fruit. Furthermore, God's love for us is unconditional. It is not our performance that makes God love us. It is simply the fact that we are His kids, those He made and delights in. Deuteronomy 7:6-9 describes God's love for Israel:

"For you are a people holy to the LORD your

*God. The LORD your God has chosen you out
of all the peoples on the face of the earth to be his
people, his treasured possession. The LORD did
not set his affection on you and choose you because
you were more numerous than other peoples, for
you were the fewest of all peoples. But it was
because the LORD loved you and kept the oath
he swore to your ancestors that he brought you out
with a mighty hand and redeemed you from the
land of slavery, from the power of Pharaoh king of
Egypt. Know therefore that the LORD your God
is God; he is the faithful God, keeping his covenant
of love to a thousand generations of those who love
him and keep his commandments."*

God chooses people for very different reasons than
we do. He loves and sees opportunity to glorify Himself
through the weak and insignificant. It seems possible that
God loves us because of our weakness, like a person drawn
to care for an abandoned baby.

The independent way, living life apart from God's call
and indwelling presence, is a temptation of the deceiver.
This rejects the intimacy that God seeks to have with us
in the journey. It is a pride laden attempt to prove oneself
worthy through accomplishing something apart from
others. It is antithetical to the great gathering of all of God's
children as seen in Revelation 7:9,

*"After this I looked, and there before me was a
great multitude that no one could count, from every
nation, tribe, people and language, standing before
the throne and before the Lamb. They were wearing
white robes and were holding palm branches in
their hands."*

As much as escapism, and off-grid living is somewhat of a popular trend currently, this is not where Jesus is taking His people. Instead He calls us to interdependence.

God doesn't need a vast majority to pour out His favor and power; instead He looks for a united remnant who have hearts aligned with Him. Sometimes as in the case of Gideon's army, God will reduce an army of thousands to a few hundred who carry the characteristics He wants to highlight for His glory. In Judges 7:5,7 "Gideon took the men down to the water. There the LORD told him, "'Separate those who lap the water with their tongues as a dog laps from those who kneel down to drink.' ... The LORD said to Gideon, 'With the three hundred men that lapped I will save you and give the Midianites into your hands. Let all the others go home.'" This is the power of partnership that submits to God and allows His purpose to become our way.

We receive life from Him and offer that life to those around us. Connection is essential; disconnect isolates and leaves us more susceptible to our enemy. War is full of chaos, with forces attempting to divide and isolate enemies in order to capture or kill; spiritual war operates with the same guiding principles. This is why connection and a united focus are necessary for victory. Just as Americans during the world wars, united, sacrificed, and experienced victory by their focused efforts, so the body of Christ must follow this example in order to win the spiritual war and advance the victory of Jesus. Prioritizing connection and sacrificing for unity serves to fulfill the mission of King Jesus. This overwhelms the forces of darkness, bringing the order of the Kingdom of Heaven to earth. Our enemy's war strategy is to steal, kill, and destroy. The Bride thwarts that strategy by depending on God and uniting to one another. Holy Spirit will do great things through us, our family, church, and nation as we submit to Him. God wants flourishing. This flourishing cascades through unity.

CHAPTER 2

Tactics of the Enemy; Lies, Isolation, and the Victim Spirit

Our enemy, satan, knows that we have great power. This is a major threat, so he pours lies into our lives in order that we would fail to reach the potential and destiny of God for our lives. When God's people unite, the enemy's evil agenda suffers incredible losses. The enemy has no problem with unity when the result is stagnated spirituality, going through the motions, or better yet, death and destruction. Jesus unveils the enemy's agenda, "to steal and kill and destroy" (John 10:10a).

Genesis 3:1-13 records satan applying his methods on Adam and Eve. He tempts with lies, seeking partnership, then he can steal. With Adam and Eve, satan questioned the goodness of God, lured Adam and Eve to partner with distrust, and this allowed satan to break their true identity.

"He said to the woman, 'Did God really say, 'You

*must not eat from any tree in the garden'?' The
woman said to the serpent, 'We may eat fruit from
the trees in the garden, but God did say,' 'You must
not eat fruit from the tree that is in the middle of
the garden, and you must not touch it, or you will
die.' ' 'You will not certainly die,' the serpent said
to the woman. 'For God knows that when you eat
from it your eyes will be opened, and you will be
like God, knowing good and evil.'" (Genesis 3:1-5)*

The enemy sowed a lie and tempted them to act on
it, this would provide him the legal access to usurp their
power, hinder their destiny, and destroy God's original
design. Genesis 3:6 "When the woman saw that the fruit
of the tree was good for food and pleasing to the eye, and
also desirable for gaining wisdom, she took some and ate
it. She also gave some to her husband, who was with her,
and he ate it." This resulted in shame, failed attempts to
cover the sin, and a powerless, victim spirit. Adam and Eve
hid from God, laid the blame on others and abdicated the
power God designed them to steward.

*"Then the eyes of both of them were opened, and
they realized they were naked; so they sewed fig
leaves together and made coverings for themselves.
Then the man and his wife heard the sound of the
LORD God as he was walking in the garden in
the cool of the day, and they hid from the LORD
God among the trees of the garden. But the LORD
God called to the man, 'Where are you?' He
answered, 'I heard you in the garden, and I was
afraid because I was naked; so I hid.' And he said,
'Who told you that you were naked? Have you
eaten from the tree that I commanded you not to*

eat from?' The man said, 'The woman you put here with me—she gave me some fruit from the tree, and I ate it.' Then the LORD God said to the woman, 'What is this you have done?' The woman said, 'The serpent deceived me, and I ate.'" (Genesis 3:7-13)

This example repeats throughout time, albeit with new details, but the same destructive pieces. We are all susceptible to satan's tactics. Jesus Christ alone defeated the temptations of satan, lived a sinless life, and traded His righteousness for our wicked and broken nature. "God made him who had no sin to be sin for us, so that in him we might become the righteousness of God." (2 Corinthians 5:21). Through surrendering to the Savior we receive His victory, righteousness, and Kingdom.

Though satan succeeded with Adam and Eve, he failed with Jesus, the second Adam. Jesus followed Holy Spirit into the wilderness and fasted for forty days. Satan came at that physically weak point to tempt Jesus three times. Matthew 4:8-11 tells of the final temptation,

"Again, the devil took him to a very high mountain and showed him all the kingdoms of the world and their splendor. 'All this I will give you,' he said, 'if you will bow down and worship me.' Jesus said to him, "Away from me, Satan! For it is written: 'Worship the Lord your God, and serve him only.'" Then the devil left him, and angels came and attended him."

Even Jesus was not off limits to the devil's attempt to usurp power.

Until coming under the reign of King Jesus, all are

by default subject to the enemy's agenda. Once a person, family, or even a nation has their identity and purpose stolen, they become pawns in satan's game to bring about destruction. When the thief succeeds in stealing one's identity he moves onto the next phase, to kill.

In the killing the enemy unites people who have agreed with the lies he has sown, producing exponential death. This is an example of how the process can unfold. If a pickpocket steals a wallet from a man, an unjust transfer of goods occurred to the victim of theft. This man is a victim of this event, but when he becomes bound by the event, it begins to shape the way he thinks, controls his habits, and cages him in, a victim mindset is unfolding. The person operating with a victim mindset abdicates his power to the negative event, refusing to find means to overcome and create positive outcomes despite a negative occurrence. To be clear, we will face painful times in life, and some of these will take incredible amounts of time and deep internal work to overcome, but this is different from what I am describing here. A victim of theft responding powerfully would cancel credit cards, call the bank, get a new driver's license, and mourn the loss of the cash that was in the wallet. The man living in a victim spirit may follow the same actions but allow the theft to shape the trajectory of his life.

This victim mindset produces a life of pain, meaninglessness, and hopelessness. It expects defeat at every turn, and resigns to continual disappointment. The victim mindset attracts a victim spirit, a demonic presence that amplifies the natural victim mindset. This fusion of the natural and supernatural realm increases chaos and destruction. We live in a spiritually charged world; everything we do has supernatural ramifications. When one lives aligned with a lie and allows that to grow it is like a pile of food waste. As it grows, it attracts flies, then cockroaches, then rats. In the same way, the lies we believe will attract the demonic spirits. Someone living partnered with this spirit accepts the view that he has no power to change what is happening around him. He believes he has no options to impact or shift the scenario of his life in the slightest. This perspective leads to isolating and pulling away, purposely walling himself off, allowing self-pity and wallowing in negativity.

When groups of people operating in a victim spirit unite, the killing stage launches. At this point, powerless people succumb to poor choices that actually victimize others. Examples include drug smuggling, sexual exploitation, human-trafficking and organized crime. Once satan steals your morality, he will force you into systems that destroy others. His goal is to destroy all of God's children.

The antidote to this scheme is first surrendering to Jesus, and receiving love and value as His beloved. Second, we need deep connections with the community of believers, the Bride of Christ. Those who honor God and lead us to stay the course of truth and righteousness, especially as we face storms. Those who protect our backs, fight for us, and tell us who we are. It is in connection and abiding with our Father, that we embrace the sometimes challenging road of what is true, even when we only faintly hear the call. It is God's people who encourage us down the path of life, who know the challenges, have journeyed through the struggles, and offer hope of victories fought for and secured.

God wired us to display beauty that comes only from our connection, collaboration, and partnership in community. In Matthew 13, Jesus tells the parable of the sower, describing different types of soil and the ability or inability of these to produce fruit. He describes these as the soil of our hearts and that those who hear and put his truth to work will produce a great crop. The culmination of the parable is Matthew 13:23 "But the seed falling on good soil refers to someone who hears the word and understands it. This is the one who produces a crop, yielding a hundred, sixty or thirty times what was sown." Good soil is a result of cultivating truth, being in a community that helps us remove rocks, pull weeds, and pour life into the soil. If we are going to produce a yield of thirty, sixty, or one hundred times more, then we need to stay connected. We need to recognize we were born into a war. We need to stand together and fight for one another.

CHAPTER 3

Fight Fiery Lies with the Fire of Truth

Currently, our Western culture is ripe with an orphan and scarcity mindset. We live in a dog-eat-dog world, where it is acceptable, even encouraged to flourish at the expense of others. Over the past decade we have seen an increase in character assassination. This is the intentional effort to discredit and supplant a person, family, or organization through gathering flaws. This results in polarization, fear, and defensiveness. People actively push away from one another based on their interpretation of events, situations, sacred text, or simply the desire to be "right". This is the realm of our enemy. He is the king of division, the lord of distrust, the ruler of shame. He desperately wants to destroy the potential that is present in each one of us. He desires to tear apart relationships, kill connections, and burn relational bridges. This is the pervasive spirit embedded in many world cultures. This spirit distrusts people, highlights evil, and builds a case against the healthy convictions and values held.

We live in an environment of division and destruction. This is a spiritual reality that we have to identify clearly for what it is. When Adam and Eve gave their power to satan in the garden of Eden, the whole earth came under the influence of the devil and his destructive mission. In his letter to the church in Ephesus, the Apostle Paul contrasts the fullness of life believers now have in Christ, to the death of those who don't believe.

> *"And you [He made alive], who were dead in trespasses and sins, in which you once walked according to the course of this world, according to the prince of the power of the air, the spirit who now works in the sons of disobedience, among whom also we all once conducted ourselves in the lusts of our flesh, fulfilling the desires of the flesh and of the mind, and were by nature children of wrath, just as the others." (Ephesians 2:1-3 NKJV)*

Our world suffers from whole systems controlled by satan, the prince of the power of the air. We are either alive in Christ or dead and under the influence and manipulation of our enemy. Our world is riddled with malevolent spirits. But Jesus brings good news through His death and resurrection. God's children have access to His power and authority, and are able to release the life and reign of King Jesus into the world. God wants Heaven to come to earth. Jesus taught the disciples to pray, "Your kingdom come, Your will be done on earth as it is in heaven" (Matthew 6:10). This isn't simply a nice idea; this is Jesus imploring His followers to align with His will. Empowering them in a different and better way: to rule by choosing to be conduits of His Kingdom power. Considering Heaven as a lush garden of paradise and earth largely containing dry and inhospitable deserts, God tasked His followers to be vessels of Heaven's flourishing reality. Through bringing the message of the gospel and the power of the risen Jesus we become conduits, that the watering holes of life may spring up in the deserts of destruction that we caravan through.

To be effective in our mission to bring life to these deserts, we must acknowledge spiritual warfare is real and accurately identify the devil as our enemy. Satan commissions evil spirits to plague us, like mosquitoes swarming their prey. These spirits desire to partner with us and lead us to deeper brokenness. They want to pour oil on a raging fire of destruction. They lead us to believe there are no options other than locking horns with those we disagree with, desiring to create more pain and inflicting greater wounds. They bring about ideas and thoughts that seem like, and may even sound like, our own voice and thoughts. But they are not our voice; we can often identify this because they make us feel terrible. Our enemy studies us, he knows our weaknesses, how to strike, which company of demons to send to terrorize. We are his prey. And if we let him, he will devour us. Holy Spirit, however, provides weapons that empower us to be defenders of others, as Paul exhorts:

> *"Finally, be strong in the Lord and in his mighty*
> *power. Put on the full armor of God so that you*
> *can take your stand against the devil's schemes.*
> *For our struggle is not against flesh and blood,*
> *but against the rulers, against the authorities,*
> *against the powers of this dark world and against*

the spiritual forces of evil in the heavenly realms.
Therefore put on the full armor of God, so that
when the day of evil comes, you may be able
to stand your ground, and after you have done
everything, to stand. Stand firm then, with the
belt of truth buckled around your waist, with the
breastplate of righteousness in place, and with your
feet fitted with the readiness that comes from the
gospel of peace. In addition to all this, take up the
shield of faith, with which you can extinguish all
the flaming arrows of the evil one. Take the helmet
of salvation and the sword of the Spirit, which is
the word of God. And pray in the Spirit on all
occasions with all kinds of prayers and requests.
With this in mind, be alert and always keep on
praying for all the saints." (Ephesians 6:10-18)

We have powerful weapons allowing us to stand firm in faith and stand together, guarding the backs of others as they guard ours. Jesus wants to help us identify the truth of the demonic all around us, unpacking the resistance we face. If we can accurately recognize what we're up against, and see the lies those around us are facing, then we can step into the truths needed to overcome and obtain victory. Sometimes we think we're the problem and yield to the lie that we are sinners, but Jesus put that old nature to death when He purchased us. This is a lie the enemy sows, attempting to get us to deny the sainthood made available to us through our Messiah. Through lies and shame, satan, attempts to distract us and prevent us living out our true identity. One of satan's methods is getting us to revisit or live from the past. He will flood us with pictures and scenes of shameful moments attempting to break our true identity, and get us to agree with a lie. Accepting his narrative relinquishes our power as we fail to trust and live in God's message that we are forgiven children, blood washed, clean, and beloved saints. Deciphering the spiritual warzone we live in guides us to silence the demonic voices that seek to devour us. The battleground is the mind, to live in victory we must take our thoughts captive.

Prepared soldiers do not go into battle empty handed. One prepares differently for an easy day hike and an overnight backpacking trip. A tent is unnecessary for a day hike. If the day hike turned into a backpacking trip, it would be disappointing to have neglected bringing a tent. Know the journey you are on and prepare for the trail God is guiding you to. Take time to listen, to ask God questions about what He is up to and what you need to bring. Ask Holy Spirit to reveal the specific demons you are fighting and how to break those lies.

Speak the bonfire of God's truth over yourself, especially when you don't feel like it, and when the smoldering fire of the enemy's lies cover your soul. Speak the peace of Jesus when you feel the chaos of hell. Speak the hope of our salvation in the face of hopeless circumstances. Speak the truth of our sainthood in the times of our failures. Read scriptures that are personally meaningful to you (sometimes called life scriptures), ones you've revisited regularly throughout your life and words of encouragement that others have written to you (sometimes called prophetic words). If you don't have any personal prophetic words, passages of scripture, or God-given declarations, ask God for them. God is the best gift giver!

In the midst of fire from spiritual warfare, sometimes we have to intentionally start a controlled fire to burn out the available flammable material. This prevents dangerous wildfires from taking off by depriving them of fuel. God wants to amp up the fire of your spirit through pouring the truth of His love and power over you. The enemy, always working to mimic and counterfeit the love of God, also attempts to spark a fire. He preys on your weakness, failures, and sins to set a fire of shame, condemnation, and self-deprecation in your spirit, preventing you from being effective. We will face the enemy's flaming arrows. God gives us tools to put those fires out, igniting fires of His truth over the former places of susceptibility. An important practice is regularly speaking the truth of God's Word in place of the lies and shortcomings the enemy hounds you with. See beyond your current circumstances for the future; God has generational deposits that He wants to make through each of our lives. Like our father Abraham, live for the promises that go beyond your temporal time. Rise to the position of sons, daughters, priests, kings, and queens. We are the Ambassadors of Heaven!

CHAPTER 4

The Rise and Fall of King Saul

The same demonic spirits that impacted past generations are still at work today. Unfortunately, the Bible is full of stories of people who partnered with these spirits and uncensored in telling of the destruction that resulted. We can learn from these stories.

The life of King Saul is an incredible tragedy, he had great promise, being chosen by God as Israel's first King, but his life was riddled by insecurity, anxiety, and fear. Saul partnered with these spirits and they undermined his identity, destiny, and potential. Saul was loved, revered, and even physically larger than the majority of Israel (1 Samuel 9:2). Yet throughout his life, the enemy amped insecurities, decreased confidence and stole Saul's peace. He became defiant, full of pride and it culminated in God's spirit leaving him. He attempted to earn his value, doing what he thought best, rather than yielding to God's directives. This resulted in his death and the Kingdom of Israel passing from his family to David.

The straw that broke the camel's back was Saul's compromise and unwillingness to completely annihilate King Agag and the Amalekites (1 Samuel 15). This passage is riddled with Saul's unwillingness to yield to God's way. Instead he acted from fear, pride, and his own assessment of the situations he faced. Saul disobeyed clear directives.

> "But Saul and the army spared Agag and the best of the sheep and cattle, the fat calves and lambs —everything that was good. These they were unwilling to destroy completely, but everything that was despised and weak they totally destroyed. Then the word of the Lord came to Samuel: 'I am grieved that I have made Saul king, because he has turned away from me and has not carried out my instructions.' Samuel was troubled and he cried out to the Lord all that night. Early in the morning Samuel got up and went to meet Saul, but he was told, 'Saul has gone to Carmel. There he has set up a monument in his own honor and has turned and gone on down to Gilgal.'When Samuel reached him, Saul said, 'The Lord bless you! I have carried out the Lord's instructions.' But Samuel said, 'What then is this bleating of sheep in my ears? What is this lowing of cattle that I hear?' Saul answered, 'The soldiers brought them from the Amalekites; they spared the best of the sheep and cattle to sacrifice to the Lord your God, but we totally destroyed the rest.' 'Stop!' Samuel said to Saul. 'Let me tell you what the Lord said to

*me last night.' 'Tell me,' Saul replied. Samuel said,
'Although you were once small in your own eyes,
did you not become the head of the tribes of Israel?
The Lord anointed you king over Israel. And he
sent you on a mission, saying, 'Go and completely
destroy those wicked people, the Amalekites; make
war on them until you have wiped them out.'
Why did you not obey the Lord? Why did you
pounce on the plunder and do evil in the eyes of the
Lord?'" (1 Samuel 15:9-19)*

God gave Saul clear instructions. These were the same
exact instructions that God gave to military commanders
in Israel's history, but Saul rejected God's directives. Saul
shifted blame to the soldiers and set up a monument for his
own glory. This whole story reeks of pride, arrogance, and
narcissism. The next verse is shocking given the context
that Saul is speaking to Samuel, the prophet, one who
has the unique privilege of accessing God. Saul pridefully
defends his actions, claiming innocence.

*"But I did obey the Lord,' Saul said. 'I went on
the mission the Lord assigned me. I completely
destroyed the Amalekites and brought back Agag
their king. The soldiers took sheep and cattle
from the plunder, the best of what was devoted to
God, in order to sacrifice to the Lord your God
at Gilgal.' But Samuel replied: 'Does the Lord
delight in burnt offerings and sacrifices as much as
in obeying the voice of the Lord? To obey is better
than sacrifice, and to heed is better than the fat of
rams. For rebellion is like the sin of divination and
arrogance like the evil of idolatry. Because you
have rejected the word of the Lord, he has rejected*

you as king. Then Saul said to Samuel, 'I have
sinned. I violated the Lord's command and your
instructions. I was afraid of the people so I gave in
to them. Now I beg you, forgive my sin and come
back with me, so that I may worship the Lord.'
But Samuel said to him, 'I will not go back with
you. You have rejected the word of the Lord, and
the Lord has rejected you as king over Israel!' As
Samuel turned to leave, Saul caught hold of the
hem of his robe, and it tore. Samuel said to him,
'The Lord has torn the kingdom of Israel from you
today and has given it to one of your neighbors—to
one better than you. He who is the Glory of Israel
does not lie or change his mind; for he is not a
man, that he should change his mind.'" (1 Samuel
15:20-29)

Saul's fear and insecurity are hidden by his pride. In choosing his way over God's, he attempts to assert his control forcibly. Saul did not begin his life full of pride. In fact, early on Saul experienced anxiety and self-doubt. I would like to suggest that because he never addressed these issues through finding confidence in what God had to say about him, that these insecurities manifested in pride and rash decisions later in his life. Proverbs 28:25 (TPT) "To make rash, hasty decisions shows that you are not trusting the Lord. But when you rely totally on God, you will still act carefully and prudently." Pride is an inflated view of oneself that often masks deep insecurity. With the power and expectation of being King of Israel, Saul's insecurities surfaced, and his need to assert his control often led him to reckless actions, attempting to prove his positional authority through dominance. Power reveals what is in the heart.

Saul's lack of confidence and nursing his doubt can be seen throughout his life. In 1 Samuel 9, Saul is on an errand looking for his father's missing donkeys. Saul's father, Kish, sent his son to find them because they had significant financial value. Kish values Saul and has confidence in his ability to bring the donkeys back, this is an affirmation of Saul's worth.

After searching for a while and in desperation, his father's servant suggests Saul visit Samuel to see if God can help locate the donkeys. This turns into a divine appointment where God speaks Saul's identity to him through Samuel.

> *"'And don't worry about those donkeys that were lost three days ago, for they have been found. And I am here to tell you that you and your family are the focus of all Israel's hope.' Saul replied 'But I'm only from the tribe of Benjamin, the smallest tribe in Israel, and my family is the least important of all the families of that tribe! Why are you talking to me like this?'" 1 Samuel 9:20-21 (NLT)*

Saul's incredulous response to the seer could seem humble, but in reality it is riddled with doubt. His doubt parallels Zechariah's doubt of the message of Elizabeth's pregnancy, delivered by Gabriel in Luke 1:5-25, which resulted in Zechariah being mute until the birth of John. Saul's doubt would surface again in 1 Samuel 10:20-24, when Samuel came to anoint him king in front of all the people. Saul was found hiding.

Saul's main problem is he never took to heart who God said he was. God laid before him a beautiful call. Saul's inability to receive, believe, and live into this created a space that nursed the lies of the demonic voices of insecurity, anxiety, and fear. These demonic influences led to his destruction. He failed to become the man God called him to be because he didn't cultivate God's truth in his life.

Jesus gives us an incredible call. Jesus made us ambassadors of Heaven; we are priests, kings, and queens who bring the rule and reign of the High King Jesus to earth. 2 Corinthians 5:20, "We are therefore Christ's ambassadors, as though God were making his appeal through us. We implore you on Christ's behalf: Be reconciled to God." Though we may not rule a nation as Saul did, we have been given access to incredible power. This requires that we believe what God has said, is saying, and will say. We have to cultivate His truth over us and hold to it as doubts, fears, and insecurities attack. We need to honor God's perspective above all others. Receiving God's power and vision involves humility, which is both the honest assessment of our weakness and a gracious willingness to partner with God's mission through us. We need a hunger to hear God and then to honor him by acting on what He reveals.

CHAPTER 5

Tapping into God's Vision and Power

God intends us to live with His power to overcome impossible situations, bringing these under the rule of the King of Kings. Jesus left us with the charge,

> *"Go into all the world and preach the good news to all creation. Whoever believes and is baptized will be saved, but whoever does not believe will be condemned. And these signs will accompany those who believe: In my name they will drive out demons; they will speak in new tongues; they will pick up snakes with their hands; and when they drink deadly poison, it will not hurt them at all; they will place their hands on sick people, and they will get well." (Mark 16:15-18)*

These are powerful actions. Casting out demons shows dominion over the second heaven – the realm of satan. Healing the sick and immunity from poison reveal Jesus' dominion over the natural realm. He is giving us His authority, won by His death and resurrection, so we can bring His kingdom and power that nothing can stop.

This is available to us, but we have to position ourselves for it. God opened a checking account for each of us and filled it with tremendous resources, but we have to write the checks. It is both true that the funds are available and we have to participate to receive them. Our participation breaks the work of our enemy and trains us in our identity. We become the powerful children of an all powerful Father. In some ways, what Christ has for us is more powerful than what God had for Saul. Saul's intended victories as King of Israel were a prototype or precursor to the greater government that we carry; we represent the worthy Lamb who is securely seated on the everlasting throne.

God is still speaking audaciously wonderful things over us; about who we are and who He created us to be. He beckons us on an incredible journey to live out who we are in Christ. The devil stands against this using the tools of lies, discouragement, and shame to enslave people, stealing our God-given purpose. The devil and his host, throughout history, have seen the power of people sold out for Jesus and fear this.

Stephen, the first Christian martyr, willingly followed Jesus' example, dying for the truth of God. William Wilberforce poured out his life, up until his dying days, to make slavery illegal in England. During World War II, Corrie Ten Boom built a special room in her home to hide Jews. Once the Nazis discovered this, she spent years in a concentration camp.

Reverend Martin Luther King Jr. spent his life in efforts to end segregation, teaching the unity of Jesus, through nonviolent acts, and fighting for the truth of

God's Kingdom. I believe God intends each of us to live a life that leaves a powerful legacy like one of these saints. The devil and his hoard are fighting to prevent this, using deception, fear, even boredom or annoyance to prevent us from reaching our God-given destinies. The battle is real, intense, and sometimes requires staying the course through the exhaustion of continual onslaught.

C.S. Lewis portrays the annoying attack of the enemy well in his book *Perelandra*. Angelic guardians of the heavens send a man named Ransom to the planet Perelandra to prevent the fall of Perelandra's Adam and Eve. Shortly after the planet's creation, Ransom arrives to be with Perelandra's Eve. The devil sent a demon in the form of a willing host, a man named Weston. Over the course of the story, Weston, who willingly partnered with a demonic entity, becomes increasingly consumed by the demon, until he is entirely devoured by the darkness.

Ransom's task is to protect Eve, staying with her as Weston steadily attacks her innocence and trust. The assignment is exhausting and when Eve sleeps or goes away to be alone, Ransom attempts to sleep, yet Weston torments Ransom by saying his name at regular intervals, preventing his rest. Weston's goal is to wear Ransom down and prevent him from accomplishing his mission to protect Perelandra's Eve. This fictional story presents an accurate understanding of spiritual warfare. If satan can't cause you to stumble, he then attempts to break your resolve through repeated attacks. But we are called to hold the line, resist the devil, stay the course.

King Saul's life is the tragedy of failing to believe who God said he was. Essentially, it was a failure to believe the bank account is full and write the checks needed. He didn't have to understand the fullness of his call and what was available to him the moment he was anointed king. The minimum he needed to do was to position himself to step into and humbly accept that truth. Western mindset wants to test the veracity of a thing before we comply, often running it through a logical test as a prerequisite for belief. Or we run ideas through the boxes of what we can control. God will not be boxed in and He doesn't need us to understand what He is up to. He wants our trust in what He asks of us.

Jesus does the impossible: heals the sick, raises the dead, walks on water, turns water to wine, travels through walls, casts out demons, and calms storms that frighten experienced fishermen. His disciples do not fully understand how or why. Our understanding is not a prerequisite to our faith in Jesus. Our task is, by faith, to step into what God asks of us. Whether or not we get to understand how or if something works is not the ultimate goal. Following Jesus completely and whole-heartedly is the goal. Be faithful with what He asked you to do, even if it seems wild, outlandish, or uncomfortable. Obedience produces life and the fruitfulness of God. Unfortunately producing fruit is a resisted task in a sin-sick world. As we will see, a variety of forces are attempting to bait us into bondage that steals our fruit, kills our life, and destroys the dreams of God for our life.

CHAPTER 6

Spirits that Destroy Destiny

King Saul is only one of many who the enemy led astray. Cain, Ishmael, Esau, and Pharoah have stories that reject God, partner with demons, and unleash death and destruction.

Cain

Cain was the first to partner with satan's murderous spirit.

"Now Abel kept flocks, and Cain worked the soil.
In the course of time Cain brought some of the
fruits of the soil as an offering to the Lord. But
Abel brought fat portions from some of the firstborn

of his flock. The Lord looked with favor on Abel
and his offering, but on Cain and his offering he did
not look with favor. So Cain was very angry, and
his face was downcast. Then the Lord said to Cain,
'Why are you angry? Why is your face downcast?
If you do what is right, will you not be accepted?
But if you do not do what is right, sin is crouching
at your door, it desires to have you, but you must
master it." (Genesis 4:2-7)

Covenants throughout the Bible involve blood. It is possible that God approved of Abel's sacrifice because it was a blood sacrifice, Cain's was not. Abel met the conditions of covenantal offering, Cain did not. This upset Cain, he let this fester, and gave satan an opportunity to suggest killing Abel to pacify Cain's wounded pride.

"This is the message you heard from the beginning:
We should love one another. Do not be like Cain,
who belonged to the evil one and murdered his
brother. And why did he murder him? Because
his own actions were evil and his brother's were
righteous. Do not be surprised, my brothers, if the
world hates you." (1 John 3:11-13).

Cain followed the beckoning of the evil one, willingly becoming a vessel of satan's agenda, murdering Abel. Those who please God become satan's targets for affliction and destruction.

Cain pleased satan, promoting his self-serving way, rejecting God's values. He became offended when God didn't approve his idea. God's goodness requires that we submit to His definitions. God pursues Cain, wanting his best, after he brings an unacceptable offering, warning him of sin waiting at his door. God empowers Cain to master sin. Cain could have partnered with God. Instead this is when Cain partnered with a murderous spirit. This spirit continues to seek those who will partner with it, unleashing havoc. This "Cain spirit" is unsubmissive, prideful, and envious. It defines its own terms, is insecure, threatens and kills those opposed to it. This is the spirit of character assassination. It aims to ruin a person's life, unleashing pain and destruction. God prunes us so we will grow, changing our hearts, to bring about flourishing. Cain rejected pruning and instead killed Abel in an attempt to alleviate the tension of his willful disobedience.

The Cain spirit wants society to validate its choices, even if these are harmful and evil. It attempts to undermine the standards of God. Choosing to change the norm, rather than the heart. Those who faithfully live in God's goodness can produce conviction in those violating righteousness simply by their example. This is God's mercy beckoning the lost. Like Cain, those partnered with evil walk with a downcast face, the result of being confronted by truth but refusing the humble path of repentance that leads to restoration.

Ishmael

At the root of Ishmael's complex story is doubt and striving for promises. Abandoning the promise of God and sacrificing faith on the altar of human effort, produced Ishmael. The "Ishmael spirit" first settled on Abram and Sarai, when they doubted God's promise, bypassed God's timing, and tried to force God's promise.

"Now Sarai, Abram's wife, had borne him no children. But she had an Egyptian slave named Hagar; so she said to Abram, 'The LORD has kept me from having children. Go, sleep with my slave; perhaps I can build a family through her.' Abram agreed to what Sarai said. He slept with Hagar, and she conceived. When she knew she was pregnant, she began to despise her mistress." (Genesis 16:1-2, 4)

We create Ishmaels through impatience, abandoning faith, and striving for results. Faith requires tarrying in God's process, reciting His promises, and waiting in the mystery. When outcome takes priority to process we birth an Ishmael.

"Then Sarai said to Abram, 'You are responsible for the wrong I am suffering. I put my slave in your arms, and now that she knows she is pregnant, she despises me. May the LORD judge between you and me.' 'Your slave is in your hands,' Abram said. 'Do with her whatever you think best.' Then Sarai mistreated Hagar; so she fled from her." (Genesis 16:5-6)

Disobedience results in pain and division. Yet, God is merciful.

"The angel of the LORD found Hagar near a spring in the desert; it was the spring that is beside the road to Shur. And he said, 'Hagar, slave of Sarai, where have you come from, and where are you going?' 'I'm running away from my mistress Sarai,' she answered. Then the angel of the LORD told her, 'Go back to your mistress and submit to her.'" (Genesis 16:7-9)

God hears Hagar, reveals Himself as El Roi–the God who sees–and directs her to return. God corrects Hagar for provoking Sarai and directs her to reconcile by humble submission. God leads Hagar back to face that messy family system that arguably victimized her, and Abram and Sarai have to face the consequences of their unbelief. God will not dismiss nor sweep this mess under the rug. Instead He brings it into the open, requiring all parties to clean it up. God uses your mistakes to shape you. He is not hindered by them, though waiting for the promises of God is far better. This story shows God's great faithfulness and redemption.

> *"The angel added, 'I will increase your descendants*
> *so much that they will be too numerous to count.'*
> *The angel of the LORD also said to her: 'You*
> *are now pregnant and you will give birth to a son.*
> *You shall name him Ishmael, for the LORD has*
> *heard of your misery. He will be a wild donkey*
> *of a man; his hand will be against everyone and*
> *everyone's hand against him, and he will live in*
> *hostility toward all his brothers.' She gave this*
> *name to the LORD who spoke to her: 'You are the*
> *God who sees me,' for she said, 'I have now seen*
> *the One who sees me.'" (Genesis 16:10-13)*

Though God sees Hagar, Ishmael lived in the deep pain of rejection which produced a hostile and unruly victim spirit. Ishmael is a byproduct of Abram and Sarai's inability to embrace the mystery of how God would produce a child in the impossible situation of people past the age of childbearing. Instead they leaned into their need for control and did not trust God. These conditions invite a victim spirit. The Ishmael spirit is an orphan spirit that strives for significance.

It feels unwanted and illegitimate. It is distrusting and fiercely independent. It is aggressive, unsettled, and seeks power to justify its existence. Conceived in doubt, it is conceptually misaligned attempting to force God's will. God wants the best for the Ishmael stories in the world and seeks to redeem victims. However, redemption comes through submission to faith that trusts God, not through one's effort to fix a broken situation.

In Galatians, Paul states Ishmael is the son of striving, a faithless, legal effort to perform. Isaac is the son of promise who comes by faith.

> "*His son by the slave woman was born according to the flesh, but his son by the free woman was born as the result of a divine promise. These things are being taken figuratively: The women represent two covenants. One covenant is from Mount Sinai and bears children who are to be slaves: This is Hagar. ... Now you, brothers and sisters, like Isaac, are children of promise. ...Therefore, brothers and sisters, we are not children of the slave woman, but of the free woman.*" (Galatians 4:23-24, 28, 31)

Issac was a firstfruit of the impossible life of faith that Jesus extends to us. God wants us to choose faith, trusting Him for wild possibilities, and reject striving for significance. Faithful submission is the way to life, abundance, and goodness. Trusting His impossible promises produces the beauty of His Kingdom. When we fail to understand God's goodness toward us, like Esau, we miss the bounty God has prepared for us.

Esau

Tension marked Rebekah's pregnancy, as Esau emerged from the womb, Jacob grabbed his heel.

> *"'The babies jostled each other within her, and she said, 'Why is this happening to me?' So she went to inquire of the LORD. The LORD said to her, 'Two nations are in your womb, and two peoples from within you will be separated; one people will be stronger than the other, and the older will serve the younger.'" (Genesis 25:22-23)*

In that culture, the firstborn male received a double portion inheritance, this wealth, status, and power came with the charge to further the family's prosperity. Issac inherited Abraham's wealth, and Esau was next. Esau disregarded the birthright.

> *"Once when Jacob was cooking some stew, Esau came in from the open country, famished. He said to Jacob, 'Quick, let me have some of that red stew! I'm famished!' (That is why he was also called Edom.) Jacob replied, 'First sell me your birthright.' 'Look, I am about to die,' Esau said. 'What good is the birthright to me?' But Jacob said, 'Swear to me first.' So he swore an oath to him, selling his birthright to Jacob. Then Jacob gave Esau some bread and some lentil stew. He ate and drank, and then got up and left. So Esau despised his birthright." (Genesis 25: 29-34)*

Esau did not protect what God valued, this is a recipe

for disaster. In Matthew 25, Jesus tells a parallel story, the parable of the talents. A master distributes five talents, two talents, and one talent to three servants. Those given five and two double these for their master and he applauds their work. The servant with one talent despises his master.

> *"Then he who had received the one talent came and said, 'Lord, I knew you to be a hard man, reaping where you have not sown, and gathering where you have not scattered seed.' And I was afraid, and went and hid your talent in the ground. Look, [there] you have [what is] yours.' "But his lord answered and said to him, 'You wicked and lazy servant, you knew that I reap where I have not sown, and gather where I have not scattered seed.' So you ought to have deposited my money with the bankers, and at my coming I would have received back my own with interest.' Therefore take the talent from him, and give [it] to him who has ten talents.' For to everyone who has, more will be given, and he will have abundance; but from him who does not have, even what he has will be taken away." (Matthew 25: 24-29 NKJV)*

Jesus wants the gifts He gives to multiply. We misunderstand God and His gifts if we disregard them and fail to bring increase. Esau and the lazy, wicked servant failed to value and apply their gifts. Both were fickle, hiding or easily giving up things which would not be returned. Stewardship requires understanding our gifts and using them to bring honor to God.

Esau's care for his birthright was so weak that in hunger, he sold it. The Hebrew word describing Esau as "faint", indicates he was tired not starving. The same word describes Gideon's army in Judges 8:4 as they pursue the Midianites. They stopped at two towns requesting bread, yet twice denied march on. Since the army kept marching, Esau's hunger seemed more inflated and lazy. He traded his future for momentary satiation. The Esau spirit trades generational impact for the desire of a moment. A reactive mindset, entitled, lacking vision, discipline, and sacrifice now for a bountiful future. "See that no one is sexually immoral, or is godless like Esau, who for a single meal sold his inheritance rights as the oldest son." (Hebrews 12:16). The lives of Esau and the wicked servant end poorly. "And cast the unprofitable servant into the outer darkness. There will be weeping and gnashing of teeth." (Matthew 25:30).

Pharaoh

Pharaoh's life is full of pride, a steadily hardening heart, willingly rejecting God, leading to his destruction.

> *"The enemy boasted, 'I will pursue, I will overtake them. I will divide the spoils; I will gorge myself on them. I will draw my sword and my hand will destroy them.' But you blew with your breath, and the sea covered them. They sank like lead in mighty waters." (Exodus 15:9-10)*

Destruction comes with satan's pride filled, self-orientation. God attempted to reach Pharaoh through the plagues. Pharaoh feigned compliance, always counter offering God's conditions for his own. Pharaoh became so fixated on his way that God allowed him eternal separation, the result of rejecting God. God pursues us and, like

Pharoah, we can reject God forever. So choose life that you might live (Deuteronomy 30:19), and today while you hear the truth do not harden your heart (Hebrews 3:15).

Though the destructive power of divisive spirits is legitimate, remember that Holy Spirit in you is stronger. Jesus is able to restore any person or broken situation. It is necessary to cultivate space for His redemption especially when hearing accusations that condemn others.

Being held accountable to our choices is necessary, but always with the grace that Jesus willingly extends. Follow His example, lovingly interceding for others to encounter truth. Christians are beacons of light who instill hope and expose evil. Christ guides us to honest conversations about our choices, including dismantling the lies that we live under. "Salt is excellent for seasoning. But if salt becomes tasteless, how can its flavor ever be restored? Your lives, like salt, are to season and preserve. So don't lose your flavor, and preserve your peace in union with one another." (Mark 9:50 TPT). Salt creates a protective shield. Resisting evil and preventing the spread of wickedness is a part of following Jesus. Resist the devil, in our lives and in the spheres of influence where God plants us. We may upset people by the way we live, Jesus modeled this and it cost His life. Being nice is not a fruit of the Spirit, therefore, allow Holy Spirit to use you to convict the world of sin. Salt also adds flavor that enhances. We add flavor to culture through living in the goodness of God. We shine light, calling out the good that God has sown in others, and encouraging the truth of the Kingdom of God already at work in others.

Steeped in pride and self promotion, Cain, Ishmael, Esau, and Pharoah rejected God. God offers us freedom to choose his loving pursuit. Without choice, love cannot be genuine. Eternal separation results from a defiant rejection of God. Christ willingly receives the humble, though broken, and resurrects life. He invites conversation, but doesn't waver from truth, clearly identifying good from evil. The spirit of Cain acts in murder, but Christ embraces those who make wrong choices. Jesus offers forgiveness and rescue from broken cycles. Because He loves, He refines us. The spirit of Ishmael lives from rejection, but Christ runs to the rejected. He dismantles lies, heals us, speaks truth, and provides grace for process. The spirit of Esau devalues, but Christ pours value into us. He engages the defiant, extending true life. The spirit of Pharaoh is selfish, but Jesus humbled himself, dying on a cross, to redeem the world that He made. Jesus stands ready to transform us, from a life of sin to truth. Rejecting people because of failed performance does not demonstrate the hope of the gospel. Jesus knew we would fail. His standard is a total surrender to Him, leading to faith that produces life.

The Pharisees once accused Jesus of driving out demons because He had a demon in Him. Matthew 12:25 "Jesus knew their thoughts and said to them, "Every kingdom divided against itself will be ruined, and every city or household divided against itself will not stand." Jesus invites us to root out the divides within, the lies and destructive spirits we've partnered with. Invite Holy Spirit to prune you, and cause your flourishing.

CHAPTER 7

Overcoming the Tactics of the enemy

Our adversary is a military opponent, commanding his forces of darkness in missions that unleash chaos, destruction, and pain to every person on this planet. He aims to break God's order and goodness. Isolation is a major weapon the enemy uses. He separates people from sources of life: caring communities, valuable friendships, and meaningful work. He attempts to isolate us in our thoughts, where he can pour a flood of sewage - lies, doubts, and undermining questions over us. Aiming to break us down and imbed lies deep within, and corrupt our thoughts and actions.

Accusation is another common weapon, when the enemy builds a case against. The serpent posing undermining questions about God to Eve is an example of accusation and character accusation. He is crafty and subtle, only utilizing bold and obvious manipulations as a last resort. He weaves a lie into the truth, giving an illusion of what is right. He inserts doubt, sows dissension and distrust, driving wedges between people. Though you can collect evidence about a person based on the fruit you can see, don't partner with him by condemning people.

God does not treat us by our outward appearance alone. We are incredibly complex, the news clip, Tweet, or TikTok video you watched doesn't give the full story. Seeking God's heart through intercession extends His love and perspective to one another. Jesus gives us His heart of compassion, leading us to encourage, speak life, desire redemption, and declare restoration over broken situations and people. Each of us carries beautiful gifts and attributes. These are the gold nuggets of God's beauty that He created us with. Some of the nuggets are obvious, others must be mined out through encouragement. The bad qualities seek attention, it's easy to call out the blaring brokenness. Instead, do the hard work of discernment to call out the gold, shining light on the budding beauty. Contend for people, don't dismiss them. Love does not disregard another, instead attempts to sort through the questions and concerns. Love holds uncomfortable tensions and fights for the gold in people. "Whoever does not love does not know God, because God is love." (1 John 4:8).

Jesus warns, "Do not judge, and you will not be judged. Do not condemn, and you will not be condemned. Forgive, and you will be forgiven." (Luke 6:37). We contend for each other first through humbling ourselves and getting in the right order, then we can help others. As Jesus says,

> *"Why do you look at the speck of sawdust in your brother's eye and pay no attention to the plank in your own eye? How can you say to your brother, 'Brother, let me take the speck out of your eye,' when you yourself fail to see the plank in your*

own eye? You hypocrite, first take the plank out of
your eye, and then you will see clearly to remove
the speck from your brother's eye." (Luke 6:41-42)

Bring correction, with love and humility, from the sobering reality that we also need correction. Our enemy flutters ideas through our minds, laced with anger, self-righteousness, and pride. He wants us to condemn others. Jesus empowers a better way. As Jesus endures the excruciating torture of the cross, our King forgives those killing Him. "When they came to the place called the Skull, there they crucified him, along with the criminals—one on his right, the other on his left. Jesus said, 'Father, forgive them, for they do not know what they are doing.' And they divided up his clothes by casting lots." (Luke 23:33-34). In the moment of the most outrageous human rights violation of history, Jesus forgives. Nobody has ever been as wholly innocent or as greatly violated as Jesus. This is the most heinous, atrocious, and despicable event in all of human history. Jesus had every right to condemn but instead He created a way for His murderers to enter God's Kingdom.

When atrocity and evil abound, follow the Messiah, forgive. Forgiveness doesn't abdicate God's government, instead it instills it. Don't give up on others. Even murderers, the sexually broken, and politically incorrect cannot be categorized deserving condemnation and treated as such. Love looks different. Paul writes this of love, "does not dishonor others, it is not self-seeking, it is not easily angered, it keeps no record of wrongs." (1 Corinthians 13:5). Love shifts the way we respond. Love invites willful compassion, instead of hateful reaction. Instead love looks deep into a person's story, finding the source that causes evil and extends grace for healing, redemption, and beauty.

We will encounter people and situations that will cause us to struggle to love, not knowing how to respond, but that's okay. Ask God how to respond and ask questions to support loving well. I wonder what would have happened had Eve told the serpent: let's ask God about these questions you've raised. I believe the outcome could have been different if she followed the advice in Proverbs 3:5-6: "Trust in the Lord with all your heart and lean not on your own understanding, in all your ways submit to Him and He will make your paths straight.". God stands ready for our questions, helping us to love. Remember to lean into Him, when you face the unknowns.

Our enemy wants our disobedience to be easy. He works diligently to entice us to sin. Be on your guard. 1 Peter 5:8-9, "Be self controlled and alert. Your enemy the devil prowls around like a roaring lion looking for someone to devour. Resist him, standing firm in the faith, because you know that your brothers throughout the world are undergoing the same kind of sufferings." We have to stay on guard protecting ourselves and others. Understanding the basic tactics of the enemy including fear, slander, and jealousy, help us identify attacks as they come. Be aware of the feelings that thoughts and ideas produce. Generally fear and negativity come from the enemy.

God is not looking for lone soldiers on the battlefield who attempt great individual feats, conquering enemy outposts, for their own glory. He doesn't want us to build monuments to ourselves through our accomplishments. Instead, He aims to unite a company of powerful soldiers, laid down lovers of Jesus. Those who soak in His presence, receive His love, and surrender to His purposes. This is the way of life. We pour out what He has poured in and we love a broken world through being conduits of His love. Paul encourages,

> *"And I am convinced that nothing can ever separate us from God's love. Neither death nor life, neither angels nor demons, neither our fears for today nor our worries about tomorrow—not even the powers of hell can separate us from God's love. No power in the sky above or in the earth below—indeed, nothing in all creation will ever be able to separate us from the love of God that is revealed in Christ Jesus our Lord." (Romans 8:38-39)*

Love dismantles the agenda of the enemy, love cannot be stopped.

The greater our experience with God, the quicker it will be for us to recognize evil. More time with Jesus helps us see what is counterfeit. Bankers recognize counterfeit currency because they train exclusively with authentic bills. This is true with God. If we get a "something doesn't feel right" sense in a situation, pray and listen for God to clearly guide you. Intimate relationship with God is our protection and our path to full life.

Holy Spirit lives in you! He is the commander on the battlefield, our friend with insight for victory. He is the unfair advantage that Jesus foretold.

> *"But I tell you the truth: It is for your good that I am going away, the Counselor will not come to you; but if I go, I will send him to you. But when he, the Spirit of truth, comes, he will guide you into all truth. He will not speak on his own; he will speak only what he hears, and he will tell you what is yet to come. He will bring glory to me by taking*

from what is mine and making it known to you."
(John 16:7,13-15)

We cannot afford to be against each other; our enemy is looking for ways to destroy each of us individually. Enforcing God's victory comes through unity, that recognizes God's flourishing is for the Bride. Stand firm and collectively thwart the attack of the enemy. If we are against one another, we risk following Judas' example, betraying others for personal gain. Judas devalued Jesus, giving up years of intimacy for an insignificant amount of money. The devil offers us the same deal: trade your sister or brother for a momentary gain. Accepting this temptation severs the body, stabbing ourselves in the back. This momentary gain, like Esau's stew, will leave us dissatisfied.

Commitment to one another requires authenticity. Ananias and Sapphira lied in an attempt to gain status, seeking the credit and praise of people. Their feigned generosity resulted in their deaths.

> *"Now a man named Ananias, together with his*
> *wife Sapphira, also sold a piece of property. With*
> *his wife's full knowledge he kept back part of the*
> *money for himself, but brought the rest and put*
> *it at the apostles' feet. Then Peter said, 'Ananias,*
> *how is it that Satan has so filled your heart that*
> *you have lied to the Holy Spirit and have kept for*
> *yourself some of the money you received for the*
> *land? Didn't it belong to you before it was sold?*
> *And after it was sold, wasn't the money at your*
> *disposal? What made you think of doing such*
> *a thing? You have not lied to men but to God.'"*
> *(Acts 5:1-4)*

Their deaths point to the sobering truth of Proverbs

21:2, "A person may think their own ways are right, but the LORD weighs the heart." It wouldn't have been wrong for them to sell the field and only give a portion of the profit. The issue wasn't money, it was an issue of heart.

As we soak in God's love we become like Him and desire to extend His love to the body. This love naturally leads to unity, especially as we sacrifice and fight for the Bride, freely giving for collective flourishing. The early church, especially Barnabas, modeled genuine sacrificial generosity, which is a key attribute of a healthy Bride.

> *"All the believers were one in heart and mind. No one claimed that any of his possessions was his own, but they shared everything they had. With great power the apostles continued to testify to the resurrection of the Lord Jesus, and much grace was upon them all. There were no needy persons among them. For from time to time those who owned lands or houses sold them, brought the money from the sales and put it at the apostles feet, and it was distributed to anyone as he had need. Joseph, a Levite from Cyprus, whom the apostles called Barnabas (which means Son of Encouragement), sold a field he owned and brought the money and put it at the apostles' feet." (Acts 4:32-37)*

Barnabas' action provides a stark contrast to those of Judas, Ananias and Sapphira, who attempted to gain approval for themselves through actions that others witnessed. The early church modeled Acts 20:35, "It is more blessed to give than to receive". Paul and Silas also lived this radical, sacrificial generosity while in prison.

> *"Suddenly there was such a violent earthquake that the foundations of the prison were shaken. At*

*once all the prison doors flew open, and everyone's
chains came loose. The jailer woke up, and when
he saw the prison doors open, he drew his sword
and was about to kill himself because he thought
the prisoners had escaped. But Paul shouted, 'Don't
harm yourself! We are all here!'" (Acts 16:26-28)*

They stayed because they wanted the jailer to hear the gospel and receive the salvation of Jesus. They were willing to suffer, recognizing an opportunity for a man's salvation. They wanted God to gain a child more than personal freedom.

Unity looks like hearts fully committed to Jesus' vision. Jesus hates pride, which caused satan's fall and the division that results from it. Ezekiel unpacks the story,

*"You were anointed as a guardian cherub, for so
I ordained you. You were on the holy mount of
God; you walked among the fiery stones. You were
blameless in your ways from the day you were
created till wickedness was found in you. Through
your widespread trade you were filled with
violence, and you sinned. So I drove you in disgrace
from the mount of God, and I expelled you,
guardian cherub, from among the fiery stones. Your
heart became proud on account of your beauty,
and you corrupted your wisdom because of your
splendor. So I threw you to the earth; I made a
spectacle of you before kings." (Ezekiel 28:14-17)*

Jesus addresses pride, modeling servant leadership and correcting the disciples who argued about who is the greatest. "Anyone who wants to be first must be the very last, and the servant of all." (Mark 9:35). Jesus witnessed pride turn Lucifer's heart, destroying his beauty and God-given purpose.

> *"How you are fallen from heaven, O Lucifer, son of the morning! [How] you are cut down to the ground, You who weakened the nations! For you have said in your heart: 'I will ascend into heaven, I will exalt my throne above the stars of God; I will also sit on the mount of the congregation On the farthest sides of the north; I will ascend above the heights of the clouds, I will be like the Most High.' Yet you shall be brought down to Sheol, To the lowest depths of the Pit." (Isaiah 14:12-15 NKJV)*

Jesus mourned pride, the destructive attempt to elevate by putting down another. Jesus modeled humble self-sacrifice, the antidote to pride, revealing humility is essential to defeat the enemy.

CHAPTER 8

Conflict, Boundaries, and Transition

A single company of soldiers cannot travel in opposite directions. The body of Christ is united in overall mission, but made up of companies heading out on different assignments. God's Kingdom is an incredible but sometimes tense, symphony of multiple parts in simultaneous motion. Jesus' desire for unity in His Bride is to see her flourish.

Unity is complex, it requires more than being in the same room together. Though Judas Iscariot spent ample time with Jesus, years immersed in the presence of God in the flesh, Judas betrayed Jesus. You can be in the same space with others and not achieve unity. It requires having the same focus, heartbeat, and alignment with King Jesus. Our focus on Jesus, our true North, will bring about our alignment with one another, like all instruments tuning to the same tuning fork. Effort spent connecting, worshiping, and focusing on King Jesus will unite the body of Christ.

Unity requires we hold clear and firm boundaries to

ensure our alignment with Jesus. Sometimes closeness, even in the body of Christ, is unhealthy and potentially harmful because we all have areas of our lives that have yet to come under the rule and reign of King Jesus. Pursuing unity requires boundaries, even limiting interactions with others to preserve relationships. We need to keep peace with others, which at times requires avoiding volatile conversations, and trusting God to shape each of us in areas of disagreement.

Jesus receives us and loves us fully and He unroots lies that are active in our lives. When we normalize and submit to lies it prevents us from the fullness that Jesus has for us. Jesus lovingly addresses areas that are not aligned but I still have the choice if I will submit to Him. If I reject His truth, I have become toxic. Jesus extends love and redemption, but boundaries are necessary so that my toxicity doesn't harm the body of Christ. If I choose a fraction of what Jesus has for me and you choose to go after all of it, then you have to create distance from me. You have to prioritize your connection with Jesus. For example, if I frequently use foul language and normalize this, you may limit the amount of time we spend together, if I'm unwilling to change. God loves us both, but my language creates an environment that doesn't allow your flourishing, so your boundary protects your heart and still gives me freedom to make a choice. You haven't rejected me but you have created healthy levels of connection, maybe you'll spend thirty minutes with me but no more because that's when things start feeling toxic. When Christians normalize sinful and rebellious perspectives, we need to draw boundaries of truth to protect us from evil. We do this in order to keep healthy access for a relationship.

When I was seventeen, my parents divorced. This was intensely painful. Prior to divorce our family lived stressful and emotionally fraying years. My dad is a beautiful yet deeply wounded lover of Jesus. He medicated pain with terrible vices. So I created boundaries, limiting my contact. This was a self-protective response, often our instinctive reactions, especially in the midst of trauma are Holy Spirit caring for us. I could not change my dad, he made choices that were unsafe. By distancing myself, I protected the potential for a healthy relationship in the future. We continue to improve our relationship, the boundary created the possibility for meaningful connection now.

Distance, separation, and warning others are healthy actions that Jesus leads us in. Paul gives this instruction about divisive people, "Warn a divisive person once, and then warn them a second time. After that, have nothing to do with them. You may be sure that such people are warped and sinful; they are self-condemned." (Titus 3:10-11). A divisive person aims to break up the good things of God, we need to warn, then stay away from these people if they continue to choose division, they isolate themselves. Paul even provides this correction for those who blaspheme, "Among them are Hymenaeus and Alexander, whom I have handed over to Satan to be taught not to blaspheme." (1 Timothy 1:20). Paul is willing for them to experience hardship from satan to correct their course.

Jesus, speaking to the church of Laodicea says, "So, because you are lukewarm—neither hot nor cold—I am about to spit you out of my mouth. ... Those whom I love I rebuke and discipline. So be earnest and repent." (Revelation 3:16,19). Jesus calls for repentance, refusal will result in the forcible removal of the lukewarm. Sometimes we need a forceful rebuke in the present so that we can gain full eternal life. Though hard to accept for the Lamb-centric view of Christianity, Jesus is also the Lion. He will tear your heart with the claw to get you to bleed for what He bleeds for. He loves us and will even use pain to guide us to repentance and redemption.

Separation can apply pain that actually catalyzes unity. When we hold lines, what is in the heart rises to the surface. Separation is an attempt to bring a person to the valley of decision having to choose Jesus or self. Love requires boundaries, admonishment, and distance. Both to maintain health and hold lines that force a definitive hot or cold response. Our willingness to live with boundaries can highlight an issue that needs to be addressed, causing one to seek God for resolution. God utilizes us to encourage people toward Him.

Often we think of toxic people as those actively choosing to be mean-spirited and partnering with evil, which is sometimes true. Other times toxicity is the fruit of a problem we are avoiding or one we haven't even identified. This is where grace comes in, to love, encourage, and speak truth. Let Holy Spirit work with those around us, letting go of our desire to fix. We can't fix anybody. At times we will need to create significant distance from a toxic person, family, or church. Potentially even cutting off contact. This is an act of love, warning another of death producing choices. This boundary of distance protects space for a potential healthy relationship in the future.

Boundaries, transitions, and change can be quite disruptive but we will face these throughout our life with God. This disruptive change is necessary, often when we transition into something new. The Israelites experienced disruption when leaving the desert for the Promised Land.

"The day after the Passover, that very day, they ate
some of the produce of the land: unleavened bread
and roasted grain. The manna stopped the day
after they ate this food from the land; there was no
longer any manna for the Israelites, but that year
they ate the produce of Canaan." (Joshua 5:11-12)

Forty years of miraculous manna ceased the day they entered the Promised Land. God led Israel to a new chapter requiring new ways. Just like Israel, our transitions are often a process taking time and effort to yield fruit. This process actually shapes something of great value within. God has good reasons for our transitions, whether leaving people, churches, or places. God launches us on adventures, shaping new priorities and leading us to contexts that cause those to flourish.

We make transitions following God in different directions to carry out new assignments. If God leads me to go South, but the congregation I'm a part of is heading North, I have to split so I can fulfill my assignment. I have made the mistake of wanting a congregation to function in a gifting or style that is mine but not theirs. Churches, like people, have limitations and not every congregation can offer everything. God sees beauty in difference and through uniting and using different expressions, Jesus magnifies Himself. God planted me in a number of congregations over the years, I have grown as I have experienced good tensions, they helped me mature. Many times I did not understand why God placed me in certain communities, but nonetheless experienced positive results. The purpose could be exposure or impartation of a different facet of God. We learn through what is modeled; more is caught through example than understood through lecture. Holy Spirit is a master weaver and He sees the entirety of our lives at once. He is deeply invested in us and desires that we have life to the full. He will guide us, and make connections that we can't understand. Be faithful to your current season, people, and assignments.

When God leads you to leave assignments, don't follow the mic drop culture, spouting unedited thoughts then walking out the door. This burns bridges and slams the door on future connection. In the Kingdom of God, we do not get to burn bridges. Do all to leave with honor, grace, and bless those you leave. We get to set boundaries and create healthy parameters for interacting with others. How we leave and the way we deal with conflict is an incredible testimony to our relationship with God and reveals His Kingdom.

Unity, Synergy, Alignment

God is our refuge through the battles we face. He is the source of life, and has a beautiful vision from our partnership with Him. The God who created the universe contends for you. He wants you free from all chains. He will lead you in the specific ways that break those bonds. We have real battles to fight, real enemies to thwart.

In 2017, I found myself in one of these battles while living in Sierra Leone. I was in the midst of a breakdown, demonically-oppressed, battling spirits of terror, suicide, chaos, and anxiety. I was scared. I felt like an animal backed into a corner, facing a predator. When I walked along the roads outside of town, I experienced demonic voices encouraging me to end my life. At times, I literally resisted a spiritual current that attempted to push me in front of trucks as they rumbled by. I went to bed each night feeling trapped alive in a coffin. A palpable darkness terrorized me almost every waking moment. Those three months were brutal and exhausting. My wife and I carry scars from that time as we fought for life and the promises of God. Yet we also hold the victory from a battle won.

One day as I journeyed from our village into the bush, where the red dirt roads of the palm plantation rose and fell over hills, past bushes, trees, and streams. I clearly heard from God that I was in intense spiritual warfare. I had been battling ideas that I wasn't good enough and I was failing. In that moment, God's peace and certainty comforted me. Jesus showed me that satan was exploiting broken areas in me, areas that needed to be addressed and healed. But I still didn't know how to work through these problems and obtain victory. I sought Jesus and His peace through praying, singing worship songs, running, and going for walks. Peace came infrequently and quickly departed. Yet that day as I walked, I knew deep inside of me that change was coming, I sensed I would leave Sierra Leone soon. Less than a week later, I found myself back in the United States and beginning a journey of healing. As I walked along the plantation road in Sierra Leone, the Lord highlighted a tree.

It was seventy to eighty feet tall with long umbrella-like limbs high up. Holy Spirit highlighted the base of the tree; it had multiple anchor pieces, running six feet up the trunk that came out three feet from the base at forty-five degree angles. I said, "God that's incredible; these are supports." And in my spirit I heard God say, "This is what I'm doing with you. I'm building support systems in your life so that you can grow and flourish. Without them you would fall in the storms and winds of life, but with them you will be able to withstand the fiercest storms. This may feel like a failure, but I am in the process of training you and building you up through this deep pain. Trust me."

So much happened through that intense and brief chapter of my life. God began exposing and destroying false foundations in my life in order to build firm, true, and lasting ones. Sometimes sustainable growth requires God to break the false within us, clean out those remnants, and start fresh with truth. Section I of this book aimed to help you identify false foundations in your life and invites you to journey with Holy Spirit to break the false and build the true and healthy foundation. Section II guides you in building the healthy attributes that God planted within you. I encourage you to do the hard work. My own journey testifies that health and God's goodness come through the process.

CHAPTER 9

Beauty of Difference, Power Through Tension

The Golden Gate Bridge is an iconic landmark of the United States. The unique and bold color embodies the spirit of the country, a place of new opportunity, innovation, and a melting pot of culture. In many ways engineering of this bridge, the tallest and largest suspension bridge in the world at the time of completion, put San Francisco on the map. The San Francisco skyline is now incomplete without its beauty and majesty. The Golden Gate Bridge withstands fierce conditions, both incredible winds and the power of the ocean currents. The tension of the suspension bridge coupled with its flexibility to sway, allow it to endure such strong forces. It connects communities, reduces travel time, and provides a way between two places previously separated by a large body of water.

Like the Golden Gate Bridge, differences united

carry immense power. A team of multi-skilled people can achieve more than a team of uniform, one-skill specialists. Honoring our different perspectives, skill sets, and passions is foundational for unity. Maturity requires that we gather a diversity of people in our lives, so they can support and refine us, and so we can pour into their lives. The differences express the fullness and beauty of God. We tend to homogenize in order to alleviate tension and experience comfort. We build teams of people we understand, we like, and who don't ruffle feathers. God calls us into the fullness of connection, building relationships with those like us and with those who are quite different from us. His purpose is to fully express His beauty and power, displayed through His diverse Bride.

Embrace Gifts

The Bride's diversity of gifts is a very good thing. We gain a breadth of perspective as we intentionally maintain meaningful relationships across the entire body. Intimidation and discomfort with gifts lead us to distance. God gives a diversity of gifts which He desires to operate in their full capacity, not hidden away or hobbling along, so that the entire body would flourish. Willingness to learn and interact with those with various gifts builds unity. Learning about another's experience reduces discomfort. All gifts are important and God wants them for us.

At a foundational level, I believe every gift is available to every person. Maintaining an openness and asking for gifts creates the conditions to receive them. Holy Spirit desires to give these, they are not awards that we earn through effort. Willingness to receive any gift increases our ability to relate to those with spiritual gifts that we don't yet have. Jesus is the head of this beautiful body. Our focus on Him reveals the necessity of these gifts that fuel unity and guide us to the purpose and mission of God. Being open to what God wants to do, especially in places of discomfort and unfamiliarity, is foundational for the unity of the Bride. We need humility, a teachable spirit, and an appreciation for what is different. Learn to lean into the wild things of God.

Our understanding is not a prerequisite of using what God gives us. We may have a gift that yields results but we don't understand how it works. Keep using it and learn on the go. "'For my thoughts are not your thoughts, neither are your ways my ways,' declares the LORD. 'As the heavens are higher than the earth, so are my ways higher than your ways and my thoughts than your thoughts.'" (Isaiah 55:8-9). God loves to expand our tents by stretching us as we faithfully step out. This process is often awkward and uncomfortable, we may not be able to explain what takes place, but "Whoever watches the wind will not plant; whoever looks at the clouds will not reap." (Ecclesiastes 11:4). Our growth stalls if we try to master gifts before using them.

Risk is a necessary path of living out faith. I've prayed for a great number of people to be healed, and most times, the condition didn't instantaneously leave the moment I prayed. But I applied faith. Faith is the currency of the Kingdom of God. Faith moves the heart of God, "And without faith it is impossible to please God, because anyone who comes to him must believe that he exists and that he rewards those who earnestly seek him." (Hebrews 11:6). God wastes nothing, though an outcome may be different than I desired. I've learned through willingly risking, overcoming the fear of man, and sharing God's love with a person I prayed for.

Love yields to Jesus, allowing Him to create deep connection and abundance. This is better than what striving efforts apart from Him produce. Yielding requires risk, stepping out, and trusting when we don't understand. Clarity is wonderful, but our minds cannot contain the fullness of God. Accepting God's mystery and vastness helps us take risks. God will lead us to do things that make no sense. God gives us a choice, but will our need to understand prevent us from simply enjoying being in His presence?

> *"Martha had a sister called Mary, who sat at the Lord's feet listening to what he said. But Martha was distracted by all the preparations that had to be made. She came to him and asked, 'Lord, don't you care that my sister has left me to do the work by myself? Tell her to help me!' 'Martha, Martha,' the Lord answered, 'you are worried and upset about many things, but few things are needed—or indeed only one. Mary has chosen what is better, and it will not be taken away from her.'" (Luke 10:39-42)*

This story illustrates the choice at play. Martha followed cultural expectations, striving to meet the requirements. Mary broke the norms and enjoyed the presence of Jesus.

Embrace Tension

Enjoying God includes risk, faith, and appreciating beauty especially amidst difference. Marriages often display the complexity of opposites attracting, and children showcase the beautiful mix of traits from each spouse. Tension comes in the context of difference yet that tension can be leveraged for power that releases profound goodness. Power in tension is the strength of a skater holding his partner in the air, while both complete their element. The power channeled from tension creates potential and momentum and reveals beauty and elegance of the dance. Don't run from tension. Instead, in the midst of it, ask Holy Spirit to reveal the beauty He wants to bring. Enduring hard situations creates the conditions for beauty to spring forth. God is uniting His Bride, expect tension on our journey to unity.

The way we embrace this tension matters. Deep connection results as we honor and seek to understand others. The way of Jesus requires gracefully embracing tensions for the sake of unity. Money is commonly a point of tension that can separate people, but the miser might learn something from the spendthrift, and the extravagant might gain insight from the minimalist. These may simply be different systems of stewarding finances rather than moral issues of financial management. We have all been shaped by our life stories, by trauma, parents, teachers, and culture. Through understanding a person's story and process we gain inroads for compassion and grace.

God willingly places us in environments where we shape others primarily through being present, not by what we say. "Be quick to listen, slow to speak, and slow to become angry" (James 1:19). To this I would add, be quick to lead by example, quick to pray, and patient as you wait for transformation. We simply cannot dismiss a brother or sister whom Jesus purchased for His glory. Surrendering our lives to glorify God by loving each other especially amidst tension, is one of our high calls. When resolving tension isn't going well, take a break and change tactics. Let go of the conflict for a time and focus on Jesus and His ability to resolve the conflict. Glorify Jesus and cultivate hope before the resolution comes. Praise and worship change the spiritual atmosphere.

Beauty can come through intense times of conflict. By nature we want to end pain, resolve tension, and create harmony. Yet there are times when the refining fire, the crucible of character, requires us to live in tension for prolonged periods. This is an opportunity for beauty. Just as resistance produces well defined muscles, we gain spiritual strength, beauty, and endurance through embracing the process. We live in an increasingly tense season of history, but God is using it to strengthen His Bride. Nothing will be wasted. The purest beauty comes from the hottest fires of the crucible, where the highest heat burns away the most severe impurities. Travailing effort produces pure masterpieces.

During the construction of the Golden Gate Bridge, to prepare the foundation for the towers, divers had to descend ninety feet, battling strong ocean currents. Once descended, they set and detonated explosives, and cleared the material loosened. Here they erected towers rising over eight hundred feet from the foundation to their peaks. Without refining the ground for the towers, the bridge would not stand.

Honoring difference in one another is a foundation, like the towers of the Golden Gate Bridge, providing strength and allowing the body of Christ the flexibility to withstand the harsh onslaught of opposing forces. Jesus leads us to unity, not uniformity. As the differing parts unite, the Bride becomes a powerful force.

> *"Just as a body, though one, has many parts, but all its many parts form one body, so it is with Christ. For we were all baptized by one Spirit so as to form one body—whether Jews or Gentiles, slave or free—and we were all given the one Spirit to drink. Even so the body is not made up of one part but of many." (1 Corinthians 12:12-14)*

A finger on its own, detached from the body is useless. A body of thousands of fingers is not a body at all. But a finger connected to the rest of the hand becomes useful for a multitude of tasks, such as chopping vegetables for a meal, digging a hole to plant a tomato, or petting a puppy.

Grace Builds Connection

We have incredible power individually and our connection allows those talents to flourish collectively. As each part strengthens, we provide greater support, encouraging one another to succeed in our mission. The Bride's unity brings flourishing as she releases power, love and beauty of the Kingdom of God, bringing Jesus more of the glory He deserves. In the midst of the war zone we live in, we carry the transformative power of the Kingdom of God!

Our interconnection is necessary to accomplish our mission. When we fail to think united, segregation sets in and we start valuing our gift above another's. This leads to manipulation, using others for our tasks to succeed. God gives unique assignments bringing His Kingdom, Holy Spirit ties those together gathering a beautiful Bride for Jesus. The Bride partners with Jesus, crushing the works of the devil. Some parts evangelize, some teach, some encourage, others are primarily focused on wealth acquisition to build and create infrastructure for the other parts to function and flourish. All are necessary. Failure of the whole results when parts are incorrectly appreciated. We need God's order and honor for each part to serve in His redemptive work.

Dismissing or demonizing a part leads the Bride to diminished impact. Partner with Jesus' vision of a united Bride, trusting Him to multiply what we bring. He still feeds multitudes with two fish and five loaves (Mark 6:38-44). He doesn't need us to point out the faults in others, instead He asks us to trust His greatness will shine through weakness. God walks with us in the waiting, sometimes His greatest work comes in our weakness and at our wit's end. We are all in different stages of our journey. God is okay with our mess, so long as we don't stay there. God sees the coming breakthrough and why it is worth the wait. Grace is a key lubricant that allows relationships to stay together rather than fraying and breaking. Stay the course of love, endure patiently, creating margin for others to walk through their mess, this brings glory to the King! God invites us to partnership, harvesting what we didn't plant, experiencing fullness we couldn't conceive, and impacting eternity.

Patience and a grace-filled appreciation for the maturity process aids our unity. If you disagree with another's perspective, seek to understand, and look for ways to lovingly converse about differences. Avoid statements containing "should" or "ought"; these words come laden with guilt and often convey the message "I know better, listen to me." Follow God's example and value process, though outcomes are important, the process greatly impacts the outcome. It is good to ask questions, even challenge unhealthy ideas, but do so with love, desiring the best for another. Accusation partners with satan, "the accuser of the brethren" (Revelation 12:10). Demanding answers and attempting to prove someone wrong will not bring unity, it is divisive. Attempting to understand, imparts care. An invitation opens a door to connection, but demanding a response slams it shut.

Some people create strife by comparing and disagreeing with another's expression of faith, arguing it is incorrect because it doesn't align with their own. These are personal preferences not foundational issues that God reveals in scripture. Often we make a mountain of a molehill of our preference, then wage a war that kills a relationship. Don't die on the molehill of which version of the Bible is legitimate, instead be grateful it is being read. Christians need to oppose sin and be great intercessors for sinners. My friend Nick, taught me this prayer, "God prevent that person's eternal condemnation, even if great pain occurs now; in Your mercy, bring them to You". We all need admonishment and correction. At times this even requires distancing ourselves from people who identify as Christians but are living toxic Christianity, as discussed in the prior chapter. Accusing, condemning, or demonizing, is a partnership with the enemy, using his weapons. We need grace and margin to talk about preference and difference with a hunger to seek and submit to Jesus' ways. Our conversations must be marked by humility, love, and care.

The unconditional acceptance of Jesus doesn't demand answers before offering love. Instead it cultivates grace and peace, in the midst of frustration, for lasting difference. Belonging is the foundation for growth. It is the effort of the divers working through the ocean currents, blasting and clearing the sites for the bridge towers, and creating the conditions for a secure anchor for the bridge to stand. Relationships stand on the towers of love and belonging. Through extending grace that accepts one another as we are, Holy Spirit has freedom to provide us invitations to change. God is working with everybody, He is refining us toward perfection from our deeply broken places. Seeking and saving, repairing and caring, reviving and reforming. Receiving love and the peace of God, allows us to be those that others want to be around. We get to shape people through being present with God's love and peace. The urge to change another rarely yields fruit and sometimes our words get in the way. Time spent together shapes each person because our perspectives and beliefs are on display. These times can shift misaligned parts in us, and take place without words being spoken. The life of Christ shines through us, we need not force with words what our character naturally reveals. At the same time, respect the difference and see what you could learn from those God brings into your life.

I believe intercession is arguably the most powerful way we get to impact people. Get before God, pray for the benefit of the person you have a conflict with, and let God soften your heart as well as theirs. We can't intercede well if we don't care deeply about a person. In prayer, ask for God to cut your heart with His compassion and care. Time with God allows Him to mold our hearts to resemble His.

CHAPTER 10

Hunger for God, Feast on His Love

Have you ever been really hungry? Like out in the woods, hiking for days, eating far less than your caloric needs hungry? As you hike, your mind offers pictures of things you long to eat: burritos, a hearty soup with bread, or a nicely decorated salad. Hunger is a natural response in our bodies, but it can be stirred up even when we are quite full. Successful advertising bombards us with messages leading us to want things, even when we don't physically need them. These develop a hunger in us.

Our hunger for Jesus works in a similar way. We experience a natural hunger for His Kingdom when confronted with painful news of sickness, death, and war. Deep inside we yearn for the world God intends for us all. We can also bolster our desire for the things of God. "Finally, brothers and sisters, whatever is true, whatever is noble, whatever is right, whatever is pure, whatever is lovely, whatever is admirable—if anything is excellent or praiseworthy—think about such things." (Philippians 4:8).

Being immersed in the ways, thoughts, and values of God's Kingdom increases our hunger for God.

Hunger for Intimacy

When we commit ourselves to adore, exalt, and magnify Jesus in all areas of our lives, we will bear the fruit of unity. Many churches are uniting on parts of the gospel but not entirely on magnifying the King. Some focus primarily on accomplishing tangible tasks and needs. These efforts alone, though good, can result in missing the crucial call of the Bride to worship. This requires being with, remaining in, and adoring King Jesus. The gospel certainly leads us to feed the hungry, clothe the naked, and care for the orphan, widow, prisoner, and foreigner. But it is all too easy to lean into the task-oriented parts of the gospel and lean away from the intimacy of knowing and being known by the King.

A follower of Jesus must be in position to receive from the Father as a child. As Jesus taught in Matthew 18:3, "Truly I tell you, unless you change and become like little children, you will never enter the kingdom of heaven." Little children are not valued for their accomplishments, though parents love their heart-felt, one-of-a-kind crafts. Children are doted on for their cuteness, held, coddled and loved for the life they exude, for who they are.

Jesus wants us to be firmly established in His love that has nothing to do with our performance. Jesus will certainly lead us to do works that express His character, revealing His love. These tasks must reveal the heart of the Father to His children. If we strive to earn our value through these works, we attempt earning a relationship with God. This relationship is a free and priceless gift that cannot be earned. Performing for acceptance is the DNA of religion. When we focus on worshiping and adoring Jesus, simply being with Him, the overflow leads us to administer His Kingdom. Relationship with God paves the way for the work He has for us.

Confusing the order, leads to tasks without worship. This yields the older brother's attitude in the parable of the prodigal son.

> *"But he answered his father, 'Look! All these years*
> *I've been slaving for you and never disobeyed your*
> *orders. Yet you never gave me even a young goat*
> *so I could celebrate with my friends. But when this*
> *son of yours who has squandered your property*
> *with prostitutes comes home, you kill the fattened*
> *calf for him!'" (Luke 15:29-30)*

Long ago the older brother quit seeing the work as a meaningful expression of the relationship with his Father. He believed the lie that he was slaving for his father's empire. Over time as his attitude festered, his heart lost compassion, so he lashed out with vindictive and graceless finger pointing.

This type of heart produces fruit with blemish, rot, and eventually no fruit.

> *"'Not everyone who says to me, 'Lord, Lord,' will*
> *enter the kingdom of heaven, but only the one who*
> *does the will of my Father who is in heaven. Many*
> *will say to me on that day, 'Lord, Lord, did we not*
> *prophesy in your name and in your name drive out*
> *demons and in your name perform many miracles?'*
> *Then I will tell them plainly, 'I never knew you.*
> *Away from me, you evildoers!'" (Mark 7:21-23)*

The warning is clear, it is possible to perform the works of the Kingdom yet be disconnected from Jesus. You could cast out a demon or heal the sick, accessing the power of God without knowing Him. This may seem baffling but even Judas Iscariot, a disciple of Jesus, did the works but didn't develop intimacy. "'Brothers and sisters, the Scripture had to be fulfilled in which the Holy Spirit spoke long ago through David concerning Judas, who served as guide for those who arrested Jesus. He was one of our number and shared in our ministry.'" (Acts 1:16-17). Judas is a prototype of performing works without intimately knowing God.

Intimacy Requires Focused Time

Connection with Jesus fuels the works and ways of His Kingdom. In the parable of the Prodigal Son, the Father corrects the older brother, "'You are always with me, and everything I have is yours. But we had to celebrate and be glad, because this brother of yours was dead and is alive again; he was lost and is found.'" (Luke 15:31-32). As children we have access to all that is the Father's. The Father's mission is bringing the lost home and resurrecting the dead. Jesus seeks and saves the lost. Celebration is essential; we must relish the victories!

The older brother lived under the performance, perfection drive which forces those submitted to it to accomplish more. "The accuser of the brethren" (Revelation 12:10), satan, uses this to convince us that we aren't good enough and we need to perform to earn God's time. He wants to distract us from the most essential work in our life, enjoying God. Prioritizing time with Jesus increases efficiency in the works that He has for us and yields more fruit. This is a paradox in our nonstop world. Protecting time with Jesus results in an abundance.

A relationship exists between what we set our hearts on and what we say, "For out of the abundance of the heart the mouth speaks." (Matthew 12:34). What our hearts feast on, creates the fruit that comes from our lips. Basking in the love of our Father, in our identity as His children, produces fruit. We need tanks full of the love of God, not striving on the fumes of His goodness. Even our strategies and efficiencies improve when we bask in God's love. The works God has for us become clearer. We must slow down, carve out quiet time to listen to God, read, and meditate on the Bible. Though I love sermons, podcasts, videos, and worship, even these can be distractions from the simplicity of being with Jesus. Activity masks underlying issues in our lives. When we slow, God frequently addresses these to heal us.

When I lived in Sierra Leone, I went through a very dark season, yet the Lord used the pain to begin creating key changes in me. I felt my work in our village was fruitless, I struggled with deep feelings of inadequacy and worthlessness. Time was slow. The days were heavy, difficult, and long. I frequently sat spinning my wheels, staring at this inadequacy. Jesus, in His goodness, wanted to break me of a lifelong performance addiction. I believed I had to prove my worth by what I achieved. Oddly, I never recognized this as unhealthy or opposed to the gospel.

The gospel tells me I'm a beloved child, received by my Father, who redeemed me by the work of His Son, while I was yet immersed in the fullness of sin. Nothing in this gospel says I perform myself into the love of God. Instead God provides an invitation to open the free gift of

His redemption. In Sierra Leone I had to come to a place of realizing He loved me. That nothing I did changed the focus of His love on me. Jesus began to break my drive to earn what cannot be earned.

In Sierra Leone I was shocked that people could sit, stare, and say nothing. For hours at a time. There was little chatter, no food or drink to help occupy the time. Simply sitting and being. It was the quiet of this time that God used to take me to my broken foundation, to start a process of healing. I believe something powerful exists in the silence, something God wants for each one of us. I still find myself desiring to be with God through activity, whether reading, singing, or listening to a sermon. But sometimes Jesus just wants to sit with me. To be present, with no task. "Be still and know that I am God" (Psalm 46:10a).

I frequently go for a morning prayer walk. Some mornings I cross paths with an older golden retriever. This dog makes a direct line to me, just so I would briefly pet her, and then she resumed her walk. She waits for me and refuses to continue until I pet her. I think Jesus is like the golden retriever, making what seems to be a diverted effort toward you and me, simply to give and receive love. Though it seems God has so much to keep in order, overseeing the complexities of billions of people, He takes an intentional, calculated, and diverted effort toward each of us. He deeply enjoys this! He is able to hold the world with all its complex problems, continuing to address and redeem those, while passionately pursuing us with His all consuming love.

> *"Suppose one of you has a hundred sheep and loses one of them. Doesn't he leave the ninety-nine in the open country and go after the lost sheep until he finds it? And when he finds it, he joyfully puts it on his shoulders and goes home. Then he calls his*

*friends and neighbors together and says, 'Rejoice
with me; I have found my lost sheep.'" (Luke
15:4-6)*

Each day God, with glee, pursues each one of us like
that lost sheep.

Can we stop, listen, and be with Jesus? He has
perspective and power to offer us during these times. These
are the moments when Jesus whispers great insight and
truth over me. Truth empowering me in a task, but the
priority is Him. If we fail to live in lockstep with Jesus we
chase tasks, rush through life, and possibly will not inherit
the Kingdom of Heaven.

Cultivate Time with Jesus

Just as advertisers sell us things we didn't know we
needed, we can cultivate desiring time with God. We
can learn to hunger for His presence. David modeled
encouraging ourselves toward more of God. "Why, my
soul, are you downcast? Why so disturbed within me? Put
your hope in God, for I will yet praise him, my Savior and
my God." (Psalm 42:11). We are going to hit times that
challenge, discourage, and overwhelm us. These don't have
to be the end of the story. We can motivate our souls to
crave time with God. He wants to spend time with us, time
that also fuels the tasks of the Kingdom. I don't think Jesus
ever uses the phrase "I know you don't want to, but you
just have to do it." Even if we find ourselves facing a task
we aren't looking forward to, He can provide vision that
motivates us. God has purpose, meaning, and joy for us in
His assignments. Jesus modeled this for us, "fixing our eyes

on Jesus, the pioneer and perfecter of faith. For the joy set before him he endured the cross, scorning its shame, and sat down at the right hand of the throne of God." (Hebrews 12:2).

Fixing our eyes on Jesus unlocks the fullness of life. He wants to be central as we work, rest, grow, launch, plan, and solve problems. Connection must take precedent to the tasks. Connection allows the life of the vine to flow to the branches.

> *"So you must remain in life-union with me, for I remain in life-union with you. For as a branch severed from the vine will not bear fruit, so your life will be fruitless unless you live your life intimately joined to mine. I am the sprouting vine and you're my branches. As you live in union with me as your source, fruitfulness will stream from within you—but when you live separated from me you are powerless. If a person is separated from me, he is discarded; such branches are gathered up and thrown into the fire to be burned." (John 15:4-6 TPT)*

We cannot yield fruit apart from our connection to Jesus. Cultivating time with Him is non-negotiable.

Genuine Intimacy

Intimacy is challenging, being known is vulnerable, and this is why a 'works alone' Christian mindset is so common. It produces a sense of justification without having to go into the messy realm of the heart. Are you pursuing more of God or just doing the works of God? Determine the motive of your heart by asking: do I hunger to be with God and do whatever He desires? Or am I seeking God in order to accomplish tasks, move mountains, and prove my value through performance? The latter desire, apart from intimacy with Jesus, produces a task-oriented, servant and master relationship with God. It comes out in phrases like "I just want God to tell me what to do so I can do it", "I don't know what God wants from me, so I don't know if I'm doing what I should be doing", "I just want answers from God." This leads to bypassing intimacy in order to accomplish tasks. The works of God are important, but intimacy with Him is essential.

Another way of thinking about intimacy vs accomplishment is the difference between cooking based on culinary aptitude vs following a recipe. When learning to cook, following a recipe is helpful. As one grows in confidence and experience, recipes can become a guide with freedom to change some ingredients because you've gained confidence. This is also true of learning a musical instrument. When first learning it is necessary to follow the music but over time a musician can launch from the sheet into a variety of complementary, beautiful and creative rhythms and solos. God wants us to know Him so we become like Him from our connection. We still check in with God and sometimes He leads us to follow the recipe without deviation. Dynamic impact comes when we express true aspects of God from biblical knowledge and personal experience. We become like the shepherds God desires for His people, "Then I will give you shepherds after my own heart, who will lead you with knowledge and understanding." (Jeremiah 3:15). Our intimacy with God frees Him to hand us the reins, revealing His love through the uniqueness of our lives.

Relationship is the Path to Redemption

Relationship is God's method of redeeming the world, first by experiencing God's goodness and then revealing His heart. Spend time in prayer, fasting, worship, and Bible study. Pour your love on God with no strings attached, no expectations of what the time should look like, or how to judge the success of it. Be with God and give because you love Him. Stoking the fire requires adding more wood. These are acts that God can and will ignite, but it takes trust in God's character and time for the fire to explode. You don't get to control how God ignites your spiritual act of discipline; you simply get to offer it, and let God do what He wants, as He wants. Faithfully fan the flame, pour love on God.

God is not looking for a transactional relationship. He doesn't want to be used. He wants your heart. He longs to have kids who are present, doing what He is doing. Connection without expectation. Be consistent and keep offering yourself to Him because He deserves it. "Come, let us worship and bow down. Let us kneel before the Lord our maker, for he is our God. We are the people he watches over, the flock under His care. If only you would listen to his voice today!" (Psalm 95:6-7 NLT). Make time to thank, worship, and listen to God. He wants to be pursued.

Sometimes God's goodness is questioned: why doesn't He just give us beneficial things, dropping them in our laps? But we have to seek God to get what He wants for us. He wants to know we desire Him and that we will take action, and position our hearts, not simply because He easily gives us what we want. He wants a meaningful relationship. Do you want a friend who only hangs around because you give him things? God wants to be loved for who He is, not only for what He gives. He is not transactional. He is covenantal.

If you want more and position yourself for more, you will receive more. "It is God's privilege to conceal things and the king's privilege to discover them." (Proverbs 25:2 NLT). God has hidden things for us; we get the honor of going on a divine scavenger hunt. Through the redemption of Jesus, we've become heirs, sons and daughters of the King.

> *For those who are led by the Spirit of God are the children of God. The Spirit you received does not make you slaves, so that you live in fear again; rather, the Spirit you received brought about your adoption to sonship. And by him we cry, "Abba, Father." The Spirit himself testifies with our spirit that we are God's children. Now if we are children, then we are heirs—heirs of God and co-heirs with Christ, if indeed we share in his sufferings in order that we may also share in his glory. (Romans 8:14-17).*

We will receive more from God though this may take tarrying and reaching for God, but He will come. He will pour rivers of living water into your life that will increase and become torrential, unable to be contained. Show God your devotion and He will meet you. He is a Father that loves to be with His children.

Hungering for God also means actively pursuing what He desires to give. It is good to eagerly desire the gifts of God. More times than I would wish, I have been in Christian settings where gifts that are more uncomfortable and mysterious like tongues and prophecy are rejected or sidelined. Mystery and discomfort cause some to reject gifts, experiences, even doctrine, in order to preserve comfort and control. We need a posture that embraces the mystery of God and seeks to grow through the uncomfortable and illogical. We are exhorted to, "Follow the way of love and eagerly desire the gifts of the Spirit, especially prophecy." (1 Corinthians 14:1). We are encouraged to want all that God wants for us. 1 Corinthians 12 and 13 provides context for the gifts of the Spirit, and is often interpreted as something like "eagerly desire the gifts, but prophecy is of higher value, and love is the most important of all. So if you can only have one, have love." But Paul writes this to incorporate a both/and. I think the passage means something like, "I exhort you to eagerly desire the gifts–all of them. Prophecy is important and good because it reveals Christ to non-believers and believers alike. And… the gifts are really important, but if you focus on gifts without love, you've missed it. So don't focus on the gifts alone, cultivate these with love. Don't be afraid of the gifts, these express God's love, eagerly pursue all!"

Jesus offers more than we can contain and gives more to those who steward well. Ask for all and step into as much as you can. He will build your maturity with the gifts. The spiritual gifts grow the Kingdom, stay persistent in asking. "Ask and it will be given to you; seek and you will find; knock and the door will be opened to you." (Matthew 7:7). The gifts flow from the headwaters of intimacy, seek and protect time to bask in the fullness of the Father's love.

CHAPTER 11

God Fills the Hungry

An insatiable hunger to pursue God is essential to unite the Bride. God has desires for His Bride, as a whole, and unique desires for the different parts. But He will not make those things happen. The free choice that God gives us requires the possibility of us rejecting what God desires. God is not obligated to pour His Spirit out, though He deeply wants to. God fills the hungry, "for he satisfies the thirsty and fills the hungry with good things." (Psalm 107:9). He promises to fill those who hunger for Him. Intentionally build partnerships with people who are hungry, leaning in, like a runner stretching every part of her body to be the first to break the finishing tape. This will dynamically advance God's Kingdom. Seek those who hunger for God. This may look like running to the front of the church and laying on your face, but it can also be expressed in the subtle but powerful forms of taking consistent prayer walks, regularly journaling, or lighting a candle and sitting in quiet to be with and enjoy God.

My friend found himself plateauing in his career. He scaled the ladder in a company, designed and implemented major projects. He hungered for more responsibility, to influence the future of the company. He also recognized he had a short window to make a major life transition, either rising in the company, or launching into something altogether new. He compiled some options to pursue, then approached his employer directly about becoming a business partner. The employer said it would be years before that could be possible. This catalyzed his pursuit of other options. His hunger and intentional pursuit led him to put his career and personal life on the altar.

Pursuing God may cost you everything you have worked for. Jesus gives us two parables that speak of this all out pursuit of the King and His Kingdom.

> *"The kingdom of heaven is like treasure hidden in a field. When a man found it, he hid it again, and then in his joy went and sold all he had and bought that field. Again, the kingdom of heaven is like a merchant looking for fine pearls. When he found one of great value, he went away and sold everything he had and bought it." (Matthew 13:44-46)*

Eternal life begins when we become children of God, then the life of His Kingdom infiltrates every aspect of our lives. Our entire life with Jesus is a series of selling all to gain all.

My friend's hunger for more led him to a bigger opportunity than he envisioned. God will empower what we think is a passing thought or silly idea, turning it into a life-altering change. Mary, the mother of Jesus also received a life-changing invitation. Her willing agreement with God, partnering with the mystery of something her mind couldn't fathom changed the course of history. May we follow Mary's example, "I am the Lord's servant…May your word to me be fulfilled." (Luke 1:38). Willingness leads us into the big and stretching plans of God.

My friend submitted himself to God's leading. He is a man of deep faith, very practical, action-oriented, a rubber meets the road type. Within weeks, the details of the option became clearer, yet more complex, morphing from being a partial owner of a business, to becoming the exclusive owner. This leap of faith came with a dynamic level of risk, his hunger birthed opportunity. Throughout the stressful process, God gave my friend and his wife peace and clarity. They were united on this venture, an absolute essential when making life-changing decisions in marriage. It proved to be a stretch beyond what they had asked, imagined, or dreamed.

God met, led, and revealed a great deal more for them. Without having clarity on every detail, they willingly trusted and went on an Abrahamic journey. God can lead you to follow Him into the unknown, for a purpose to be revealed when you arrive. "The LORD had said to Abram, "Go from your country, your people and your father's household to the land I will show you. "I will make you into a great nation, and I will bless you; I will make your name great, and you will be a blessing." (Genesis 12:1-2). My friends' journey still unfolds and comes with new questions to answer, but as they faithfully seek God in their hunger, He fills them with good things. God looks for those hungry and willing to risk. The fullness that He wants to build in us comes by stepping out. He works with submitted, willing hearts that leap into adventure.

In your life, the next step may not be a major life change. It could be an inkling to connect with a person, the desire to learn an instrument, or start a new activity. God looks for Psalm 51:17 people, "My sacrifice, O God, is a broken spirit; a broken and contrite heart you will not despise.". Hunger is an expression of a broken and contrite heart. Hunger drives us to satisfy longings. Hunger alerts of something we need that we do not have. God has plans and desires for our lives that require pursuing hunger even though we aren't sure how to satisfy it. Lean into your hunger, let God guide you to a Psalm 23 feast.

> *"The LORD is my shepherd, I lack nothing. He*
> *makes me lie down in green pastures, he leads*
> *me beside quiet waters, he refreshes my soul. He*
> *guides me along the right paths for his name's sake.*
> *Even though I walk through the darkest valley,*
> *I will fear no evil, for you are with me; your rod*
> *and your staff, they comfort me. You prepare a*
> *table before me in the presence of my enemies. You*
> *anoint my head with oil; my cup overflows. Surely*
> *your goodness and love will follow me all the days*
> *of my life, and I will dwell in the house of the*
> *LORD forever."*

Hunger for God and enjoying the feast He has for us can include buying a house or business, having a child, or fasting and praying for healing. Hunger opens the way to see life through God's lens as the spiritual and common collide. Here nothing is relegated to going through the motions. He shapes us through all things. What are you hungry for? What are you leaning into, contending for, extending your whole self toward to reach for God's fullness? Nothing held back, nothing comfortable or easy.

All muscles engaged to grab that good thing God has for us. It is a beautiful metaphor of how to position ourselves in every situation for more of God. "Not that I have already obtained all this, or have already arrived at my goal, but I press on to take hold of that for which Christ Jesus took hold of me." (Philippians 3:12). What practical steps are you taking to cultivate a deeper relationship with Jesus? What are you offering Him that He hasn't previously had access to? Where do you see yourself all out pursuing Him?

Jesus invites His followers to an all out pursuit of Him.

"As Jesus was walking beside the Sea of Galilee, he saw two brothers, Simon called Peter and his brother Andrew. They were casting a net into the lake, for they were fishermen. 'Come, follow me,' Jesus said, 'and I will send you out to fish for people.' At once they left their nets and followed him." (Matthew 4:18-20)

Peter and Andrew dropped all they had structured their life around to follow the Rabbi from Nazareth. Jesus has no qualms of completely upsetting the normalcy and comfort of our lives in order that we would gain His Kingdom. Compassion is sympathizing and suffering with another. We can willingly enter God's compassion, moving His heart as we choose to leave what is comfortable and embrace suffering with Him. Get some skin in the game, hurt for what He hurts for, weep with Him, orient your life to Him.

Hunger is something to pursue together. Though the concepts and ideas presented in this chapter are very individualized, these pursuits must be collective for the Bride to unite. Look for others who are hungry. A hungry spirit is a communicable attribute. The hungry unite like coals of a fire merging together that create more flames, warmth, and light. Perhaps you are a leader in a church, business, or community. Perhaps you have children or people who seek you out. Pour into them. Partner with their hunger to build a greater hunger. God wants us to know His beauty and mystery in community. If you aren't hungry, spend time with those who are. If you aren't sure what you have to offer, connect with people who can help you to identify and apply your hunger and gifts. The Bride must pursue King Jesus together, our collective pursuit brings Him great pleasure. In unity let us hunger for and pursue Jesus.

CHAPTER 12

Environments that Cause Dynamic Change

The unity of God's people sparks dynamic redemptive actions providing abundant life to our broken world. As we unite, hearing God's heart and working toward His desires, we become a conduit for Holy Spirit to bring healing to the world. Think of unity as different sizes of water supply pipe, a one-inch diameter pipe carries greater amounts than a half-inch. Like pipes, we are conduits of Holy Spirit. "And if the Spirit of him who raised Jesus from the dead is living in you, he who raised Christ from the dead will also give life to your mortal bodies because of his Spirit who lives in you." (Romans 8:11). God lives in us and we continually increase our capacity as we go through the sanctification process; relinquishing unsubmitted territories of our hearts, breaking lies we've believed, and instead aligning with God's ways. This releases more of His abiding presence, better equipping us to serve Him. Sanctification increases our capacity, like increasing the size of your water supply pipe, allowing more of God to flow through you.

Unity combines our individual one inch supply lines, exponentially increasing our capacity, to a much larger diameter. God has beautiful things for His Bride accessible only through unity. The enemy knows this and purposely sows division to prevent the Bride from achieving fullness; he fears the power of our submission to Christ. United we will accomplish more than is possible independently.

Cultural Challenges to Unity

I believe two key Western cultural mindsets challenge this collective pursuit. First is the overemphasis of production, including an unhealthy rhythm that fails to prioritize health and wellness. One example is rest comes only after completing work, yet work never ceases. That is why sabbath rest is an essential rhythm, a gift, not based on performance.

The second challenge is an independent mindset; a cornerstone of American culture. This mindset promotes and rewards those who are independently successful and don't need others. The Kingdom of God includes healthy levels of independent choice, action, and internal motivation to accomplish God's work. We are living in Jesus' redemptive zeal to establish His Kingdom, as prophesied in Isaiah 9:7 "Of the greatness of his government and peace there will be no end. He will reign on David's throne and over his kingdom, establishing and upholding it with justice and righteousness from that time on and forever." Jesus' birth launched this and His government increases daily. The core lie of the independent mindset is we are more effective independently, but God's triune nature reveals the power and beauty of unhindered unity.

Especially for Western Christians, we need to willingly adjust our individualistic mindsets, creating space for healthy spiritual practices that honor the body of Christ. This includes how we go about prayer times, Bible studies, and meals together. Discipline leads to flourishing. "For lack of discipline they will die, led astray by their own great folly." (Proverbs 5:23). Willingly choosing disciplines unlocks God's power and vision in our lives. Eating, sleeping, and workout plans, also establishing consistent time with God in prayer, Bible reading, and worship. Disciplines create structures for flourishing. The disciplines God invites us into provide means to access greater beauty through refinement.

Correction is valuable. "Those who disregard discipline despise themselves, but the one who heeds correction gains understanding." (Proverbs 15:32). Embracing correction is self-care, and unlocks the promises of God. Discipline, correction, and alignment with God are foundational for unity within the Bride. God loves you where you are, but He loves you too much to leave you there. He matures those He loves, but maturity is costly and requires that the Bride willingly step into the maturity process. Some maturity comes via compulsory means, but God always desires those who willingly engage.

Proverbs highlights some key benefits of correction. Correction is necessary for growth: "Whoever loves discipline loves knowledge, but whoever hates correction is stupid." (Proverbs 12:1). Correction prevents disaster and protects honor: "Whoever disregards discipline comes to poverty and shame, but whoever heeds correction is honored." (Proverbs 13:18). Correction is the route to life: "Whoever heeds discipline shows the way to life, but whoever ignores correction leads others astray." (Proverbs 10:17). Correction is willingly submitting to God's authority. "Trust in the LORD with all your heart and lean not on your own understanding; in all your ways submit to him, and he will make your paths straight." or "he will direct your paths." (Proverbs 3:5-6). Submission and trust of authority fly in the face of the independent mindset.

Fear and Pride: Roots of Defiance

I believe the roots of defiance are fear and pride. The fears of abuse, neglect, as well as distrust lead to this. The fear of abuse is significant because Christians and churches have abused. These painful stories require tact, honor, and grace to heal. We also need to understand what submission is and isn't. Submission primarily is to Jesus, following His lead. Submission doesn't mean I turn my brain off, quit listening to checks in my spirit, or can't ask questions. Submission is a bit of a dance, a gray area, requiring discerning who to submit to and to what degree. Submission is relational, involving trust.

Pride on the other hand is rebellion, seeking control, believing its way is better. Pride is narcissistic, distrusting authority, including God, and will not follow another's leadership. I wrote this chapter in the airport while flying standby. I hoped to get to Utah to be with friends, so I submitted this desire to God. I arrived at four in the morning. The flight at six was full, the next flight at ten was also full. As I wrote, I waited for the midday flight which ended up being full. I trusted God that even if I spent the whole day in the airport and didn't make a flight, which I didn't, He had a purpose for the time. I had a great cup of coffee and a lovely time writing. I did not understand the "why?" behind the day, but I trusted He had good for me in the adventure.

Submitting to the authority of God requires leaning into the power of the Bride over my own strength. I may have to slow down and do things that aren't linear. As the African proverb states, "If you want to go fast, go alone; if you want to go far, go together.". The independent mind believes more can be accomplished alone because one can move fast. God sees dynamic potential resulting from our interdependence. Calibrating to a pace we can all keep produces eternal fruit and prevents burnout and fruitlessness. Some will have to slow down, while others will speed up.

Four Soils of Community

Jesus tells of a farmer sowing seed, revealing the ability of various soils to produce fruit.

"Then he told them many things in parables, saying: 'A farmer went out to sow his seed. As he was scattering the seed, some fell along the path, and the birds came and ate it up. Some fell on

rocky places, where it did not have much soil. It
sprang up quickly, because the soil was shallow.
But when the sun came up, the plants were
scorched, and they withered because they had no
root. Other seed fell among thorns, which grew up
and choked the plants. Still other seed fell on good
soil, where it produced a crop—a hundred, sixty or
thirty times what was sown."' (Matthew 13:3-8)

A case can be made that these different soils are
an expression of independent versus interdependent
communities. The first three soils are independent ways
which, at best, produce quickly sprouting seeds that are
choked out. The worst is a large scale bird feeder. The
good soil is a nurturing, stable environment that yields a
great harvest.

The path, the rocky soil, and the plot of thorns may
represent fast paced, independent lifestyles that yield
nothing. The steady paced good soil yields fruit. Good
soil requires effort: clearing rocks, thorns, even chasing
off pests. It requires nutrition, compost, and water. The
path, the rocky soil, and the plot of thorns, are areas of land
that need cultivation to yield a harvest. The good soil is
an intentional community that creates the conditions that
yield an abundant harvest.

The path is hard, compacted, unable to receive the
seed, like communities that conform to the fast-paced
patterns of the world, are self-absorbed, and unable to
receive those that come to them. Rocky soil is harsh and
restrictive, unable to support the seed over time. These are
communities where rules and rituals take precedence to
genuine connection, including connecting with Jesus. The
soil with thorns creates space for compromise, promoting

alternative agendas and values contrary to the genuine gospel. These communities focus on social acceptance, bowing to evil agendas, producing quick sprouting, pseudo Kingdom crops tarnished by the world. They reject the purity of truth, don't pursue raw and genuine intimacy with God, instead producing immature, inedible fruit. The independent styles are marked by successful programming, getting through the bullet points of the service, looking polished, being right, and producing an image void of deep connection. Churches need to produce beauty, but fueled by genuine connection that willingly embraces the messy stories of broken people.

God's fullness comes through our connection to a healthy community. It is the context for our growth and pruning, is not void of challenge or friction, yet these are tempered by grace and mercy to prevent becoming hard and harsh like the path or rocky soil. Legal and religious spirits stifle growth. A gospel that lacks conviction and is influenced by the zeitgeist or hidden agendas will prevent maturity. We need structure and order rooted in love to ensure the growth of God's vision. A healthy community is deep and loving, able to have hard conversations and constructive conflict. It stands firm through cultivating the rich nutrients of the character of God, found throughout the Bible. These are essential for personal and corporate growth, and result in yielding the harvest that God eagerly longs to gather.

Individual and Corporate Evaluation

An independent mindset wants to be judged for personal performance, based on an equal standard that all are held to and this way credit can be earned by individual performance. This is somewhat aligned with the truth revealed in Romans 14:12, "So then, each one of us will give an account of ourselves to God." We will have a personal account to give. I believe we will also give an account of our unity. Take the example of Israel wandering the desert for forty years. Numbers 14 shows the aftermath of Israel's rejection of God's promise due to fear.

> *"Joshua the son of Nun and Caleb the son of Jephunneh, who were among those who had spied out the land, tore their clothes [as a sign of grief], and they spoke to all the congregation of the sons of Israel, saying, 'The land through which we passed as spies is an exceedingly good land. If the Lord delights in us, then He will bring us into this land and give it to us, a land which flows with milk and honey. Only do not rebel against the Lord; and do not fear the people of the land, for they will be our prey. Their protection has been removed from them, and the Lord is with us. Do not fear them.'"* (Numbers 14:6-9 AMP)

Joshua and Caleb scouted, heard God, and confidently shared God's invitation to take the land, but they were not spared from the consequences of group unbelief. It seems God could have rewarded Caleb and Joshua, doling out a couple parcels of Promised Land for the two faithful spies and their families. They could have been gatekeepers, ambassadors of the Promise, cultivating parcels of land while the unbelievers died off during their forty-year penance. But God does not segregate His people. We must apply faith and stand on God's promises individually, but many victories come by unity and certain plunder is reserved for the body of Christ. This requires long suffering and intentionally pursuing unity. Even pursuing those parts making anti-Christ decisions. Dynamic power flows from the unity of the whole, not just the parts willing to unite. Keep doors of connection open and intercede for the wayward. God doesn't give up on people nor can we. God will provide good things for the faithful, He rewarded Joshua and Caleb, "Not one of you will enter the land I swore with uplifted hand to make your home, except Caleb son of Jephunneh and Joshua son of Nun." (Numbers 14:29). God will give us the strength to endure negative group consequences with the promise of future reward.

The independent perspective wants the easy out of an eject button to avoid group consequences that feel undeserved. It wants individual positive efforts to shield the negative impacts of group choices. Jesus guides us to unity and encourages radical forgiveness. "Then Peter came to Jesus and asked, "Lord, how many times shall I forgive my brother or sister who sins against me? Up to seven times?" Jesus answered, "I tell you, not seven times, but seventy-seven times." (Matthew 18:21-22). Forgive each time you're asked. We may have to endure the same offense and forgive it multiple times. Genuine repentance must be met with forgiveness. Rebuild a healthy relationship and be sure to apply appropriate boundaries. Forgiveness does not mean resetting to the status before the sin, it doesn't abdicate consequences. Forgiveness relinquishes offense and seeks God's blessing for another.

An independent perspective mirrors Judges 21:25, "In those days Israel had no king; everyone did as they saw fit." This ignores the impact of our lives on one another. Jesus models unity, including intercession, standing in the gap for others. He leads us in a fixed commitment to our community, a willingness to embrace pain, shed tears, and stick through challenges. We endure to see promises fulfilled, instead of leaving when discomfort arises. Enduring difficulties and tensions produces fruit. Long suffering is a fruit of the Spirit, marked by holding fast rather than leaving over petty disagreements. Within Western Christianity is an unhealthy independent and consumer mindset, taking from church and willing to leave a community as soon as things are unfavorable. God calls us to deeper, fruit bearing investment in our communities.

Leaving Fruitless Communities for the Fruitful

God will lead people to leave communities - including friendships, Bible study groups, and churches, but this is an intentional process. Part of His purpose is cross pollination, building up different parts of the body. God may move a person full of faith from a faithless environment, like Joshua and Caleb, who endured wandering the desert and buried a faithless generation. We also may endure hardships and like Joshua and Caleb, bury doubters, before we enter the promises of God.

Unity is our aim. God's holiness requires pruning and even separation from those who are preventing us from obtaining our full calling. This can look like Jesus telling Peter that his perspective was off, or it can actually require leaving environments that are no longer growing. If a living fish stays in the Dead Sea long enough, it will die, it will not be able to revive the Dead Sea. Especially when communities have become stagnant, immovable, and rebellious. John the Baptizer speaks of Messiah as one who separates, "He will baptize you with the Holy Spirit and fire. His winnowing fork is in his hand, and he will clear his threshing floor, gathering his wheat into the barn and burning up the chaff with unquenchable fire" (Matthew 3:11-12). Jesus baptizes His church with threshing and fire. He will have a fruitful church, He will root out the fruitless, burning away those actively preventing others from producing.

Paul warns of those attempting to infiltrate to destroy, "I know that after I leave, savage wolves will come in among you and will not spare the flock. Even from your own number men will arise and distort the truth in order to draw away disciples after them. So be on your guard!" (Acts 20:29-31a). Our enemy desires to plant covert agents in our churches aiming to shipwreck God's vision. This will not be obvious like radical cults that insist on additional sacred texts and require wicked rituals. Throughout the world are false churches with the markings of Christianity. Our enemy corrupts familiar structures, slightly twisting the truth to lead people astray. Jesus will move you from a fruitless church or one where leaders' hearts are cold, no longer pursuing Him. Jesus said, "Yet a time is coming and has now come when the true worshipers will worship the

Father in the Spirit and in truth, for they are the kind of worshipers the Father seeks" (John 4:23) Jesus tells a parable revealing this about true and false worshippers.

> *"The kingdom of heaven is like a man who sowed good seed in his field. But while everyone was sleeping, his enemy came and sowed weeds among the wheat, and went away. When the wheat sprouted and formed heads, then the weeds also appeared. The owner's servants came to him and said, 'Sir, didn't you sow good seed in your field? Where then did the weeds come from?' 'An enemy did this,' he replied. 'The servants asked him, 'Do you want us to go and pull them up?' 'No,' he answered, 'because while you are pulling the weeds, you may uproot the wheat with them. Let both grow together until the harvest. At that time I will tell the harvesters: First collect the weeds and tie them in bundles to be burned; then gather the wheat and bring it into my barn.'" (Matthew 13:24-30)*

The field has fruitful wheat and fruitless weeds that look like wheat, so do our congregations. Though Jesus is a redeemer and models contending to bring people back to Him. Sometimes our contending, though important, will not shift the free will choice of the heart fixed on rebellion. God may use you to present the truth for a season and then move you. Stay until Holy Spirit leads you and then go.

All churches provide opportunities for growth via tension, this is part of Holy Spirit's refining process. The tension often causes recoil, desiring a self-protected, comfort-driven way, wanting a church where you pick all the people you like. God's way builds unity through tension, developing steadfast pillars of hope, immovable refuges. Deep investment in relationships is necessary and requires facing tension. Without it you will float from group to group. In each new situation you may face the same type of difficulty, albeit packaged differently and providing another opportunity for personal maturity. To leave a relationship when hitting discomfort is to disconnect from God. Challenges strengthen our lives, encouraging us to embrace what God values.

Submission is our heart beating to the rhythm of God's. This is essential especially when lacking understanding. Trust doesn't require understanding. Trust depends on God and community. Trust holds firm to God's assignment. Jesus provides the ultimate example, yielding His life in full trust and submission to the will of the Father. Everything Jesus modeled, we can obtain. "Very truly I tell you, whoever believes in me will do the works I have been doing, and they will do even greater things than these, because I am going to the Father." (John 14:12). Trials unite and refine God's fully submitted, powerful Bride.

United by Trials

Trials, though painful, hold power to create bonds. Challenges of all kinds provide means for unity. We were born into a spiritual war, Jesus unites His Bride to resist the assault of our enemy. God knows that support, encouragement, and care for one another are necessary to our Kingdom mission. God also knows that the enemy of our souls seeks to create division. Unity is a strategic counterattack on the enemy's attempts to divide and conquer, assaulting the forces of darkness, releasing the life of the Kingdom of Heaven.

A decade ago, my wife and I served as Peace Corps volunteers in Ukraine. It was a chapter filled with trials that matured our marriage and supplied incredible memories. I vividly remember landing in Kiev on a cold, snowy night, then traveling by bus, crossing frozen rivers dotted with men ice fishing, as we headed to a retreat center. We met Peace Corps staff and began our immersion. Due to the common challenges that united us we quickly developed meaningful relationships with volunteers. It became natural to provide hospitality, share meals, host and be hosted while traveling. Trials can unite and lead us to generosity of heart before our minds fully catch on. Jesus is building this in His Bride.

> *"They were continually and faithfully devoting themselves to the instruction of the apostles, and to fellowship, to eating meals together and to prayers. A sense of awe was felt by everyone, and many wonders and signs (attesting miracles) were taking place through the apostles. And all those who had believed [in Jesus as Savior] were together and had all things in common [considering their possessions to belong to the group as a whole]. And they began selling their property and possessions and were sharing the proceeds with all [the other believers], as anyone had need. Day after day they met in the temple [area] continuing with one mind, and breaking bread in various private homes. They were eating their meals together with joy and generous hearts, praising God continually, and having favor*

with all the people. And the Lord kept adding to their number daily those who were being saved."
(Acts 2:42-47 AMP)

God is leading us on a journey to live for each other, training us to live as one. He is shifting the way we think, live, and act, uniting us for His mission with multifaceted expression. This will align and synergize the Bride, unlocking the dynamic power of Jesus' Kingdom into our world. The power that comes from our unity in Christ frightens satan, so he has ramped up divisive tactics including fear and isolation in an attempt to waylay the impact of unity. The Bride is maturing and withstanding the storm. She is about to step into a season of intense flourishing, gathering the harvest. We are launching into the abundance of the beauty of unity.

CHAPTER 13

Synergy and Sowing Eternally

Unity synergizes the release of God's dynamic redemptive power to the world. Synergy is the power of a rowing team in unison, applying their oars to swiftly propel their boat under the call of the coxswain. Each rower focuses on the one giving the call. It requires skill, discipline, and determination to carry out an individual task that compounds through unity, benefitting all. In unity, power explodes through the effort of each rower, causing the boat to efficiently glide through the water. The beauty of strength and commitment, nothing held back, submitted to achieve a shared goal. Christ calls His body to clip through the waters as a united force.

In Jesus, we are in the same boat, whether we like it or not. We cannot operate on our own, as this will cause the boat to spin in circles, move backwards, and possibly capsize. Neither can we row in our own directions at whatever pace we want, this yields erratic motion. One rower can't do the work for all. We flounder apart from honor, support, and love.

Synergy requires recognizing what God has uniquely gifted us with and pursuing God for the context to apply it. We also get to call out the gifts and talents of those around us, encouraging and bolstering the Bride. This cultivates an environment where all gifts flourish, including our own. God gives each gift to manifest His glory. It is an honor to steward these gifts for His exaltation. Gifts glorify Jesus and are not about our justification and validation. Jesus justified us while we were yet sinners (Romans 5:8-11). We did nothing to gain value, it is a free gift. The additional gifts we receive are for the glory of Jesus. Seeking to apply our gifts for personal accolades misses their purpose. God wants the beauty, accolades, and richness that comes from our gifts to expand His glory. Attempting to hold glory for ourselves, steals from God. Gifts are means to bless His Bride, the world, and ultimately glorify God.

Gifts flourish in the context of community, our gifts mature through connection. Ask Holy Spirit to guide you to the community for your gifts to flourish. This requires active surrender, dying to self, allowing the seeds within to spring to life. Harsh conditions, uncomfortable people, and challenging scenarios can produce fruit that will come in no other way. When growing plants from seeds, one starts indoors with controlled conditions. These young plants gain strength through exposure to outside conditions. Hardening off plants is the process of transitioning them from a controlled indoor setting to planting outside. This takes weeks, incrementally building strength through exposure to the elements until ready to plant. We need to be hardened so we can endure harsh environments and respond with grace. We must mature in order for our gifts to flourish in every circumstance.

God is maturing and uniting the gifts of His Bride, increasing her impact. He also synergizes the gifts across time, combining seeds and fruit from all generations. God builds with what has been poured out throughout time. The gifts and efforts that were the ceiling of one generation become the floor of the next. God's work is seamless, everlasting, outside of the limits of temporal space and time.

Sometimes one generation contends for something that the next generation or generations failed to sustain. If your grandparents built a well, but your parents failed to maintain it, you can repair it. You have restorative work to do, but not the pioneering work your grandparents did. If your grandparents fought for sexual purity in your family line, but your parents partnered with social norms, becoming sexually impure, you can access the purity your grandparents obtained. You will have to close the door of sin that your parents normalized through their choices, but you can reestablish sexual purity in your family line.

Things which the generations before us fought for are available for us, allowing for synergy in what God was doing then and continues to desire now. In a relay race, a team of four runners each run a quarter of the distance, their collective time determines the place the team finishes in. The second runner links the first and the last two runners, but the end result is determined by the total time of the team. We have a single leg to run in God's redemptive collaboration of history, involving all His children. Paul encourages us to commit to intense training and run our leg with the team in mind, doing all to win the prize. A fast individual time is helpful, but the result depends on the team effort.

> *"Do you not know that in a race all the runners run, but only one gets the prize? Run in such a way as to get the prize. Everyone who competes in the games goes into strict training. They do it to get a crown that will not last, but we do it to get a crown that will last forever. Therefore I do not run like someone running aimlessly; I do not fight like a boxer beating the air. No, I strike a blow to my body and make it my slave so that after I have preached to others, I myself will not be disqualified for the prize." (1 Corinthians 9:24-27)*

Jesus longs for a united, powerful, and radiant Bride. He is pleased with our individual efforts, following the specific paths He calls us to, and individual rewards exist for our efforts. Jesus leads us to, "Love each other deeply, as much as I have loved you. For the greatest love of all is a love that sacrifices all. And this great love is demonstrated when a person sacrifices his life for his friends." (John 15:12-13). Jesus calls us to a sacrificial life, supporting the Bride for Jesus' glory. Living for one's own glory misses Jesus.

The runner with the fastest individual time in a relay race celebrates her time, but she will not obtain the prize if the team fails to be fastest. In the body of Christ, we can individually do an awesome job serving and living out our call. If these individual efforts are for our own sense of affirmation, and aren't tied to the mission of the Bride, we missed the reason for our effort. Our purpose is for our team to win, for Jesus to receive the full glory of the price He paid. Jesus desires a united Bride, not severed pieces.

Sowing to Eternity

Jesus stands outside of space and time, we track our lives linearly by each passing year. At the time I wrote this paragraph, I listened to a worship service that took place five hours ago, yet dynamic and eternal truth came from that service. God is eternal, true, and present. Experiencing God is experiencing the eternal. What I do today, in this chapter of my life, is active in the present, but what I do by faith has eternal impact. Investment in God's Kingdom is eternal. As Paul explains:

> "if anyone builds on the foundation with gold,
> silver, precious stones, wood, hay, straw, each one's
> work will be clearly shown [for what it is]; for
> the day [of judgment] will disclose it, because it
> is to be revealed with fire, and the fire will test the
> quality and character and worth of each person's
> work. If any person's work which he has built [on
> this foundation, that is, any outcome of his effort]
> remains [and survives this test], he will receive a
> reward. But if any person's work is burned up [by
> the test], he will suffer the loss [of his reward];
> yet he himself will be saved, but only as [one who
> has barely escaped] through fire." (1 Corinthians
> 13:12-15 AMP)

Eternal works are more valuable and worth our investment. I am panged with sorrow reflecting on time and effort sown into temporary works of hay or straw, but I am motivated to refine my approach and pursue the works of gold, silver, and precious stones. I want to sow into the eternal purpose God designed. Sometimes these are the simplest things we do.

Recently some friends sent me a message. I lived with them over twelve years ago, they had a child coming but the pregnancy was difficult and their son was born quite early. A group of eight of us gathered to pray for this child. We listened to God and interceded for this boy. We wrote down prophetic scriptures and pictures we heard God speaking over his life and gave these to my friends. Twelve years to the date that we prayed and wrote these down, they found this paper in a box. Their son is in middle school now. I had forgotten about that time of prayer but reading their message, the memory flooded back. This was an eternal investment in God's Kingdom and I received a dividend of joy when I read the message.

During that same season, a group of us gathered to pray five days a week for an hour. We prayed for growth and purity in one another, for God to reveal Himself to people on our college campus, and for revival in the United States and the world. We sowed prayers the Lord gave us. We thought so many of those prayers were about that specific time in linear history. I now have a better understanding; we were sowing to that moment and simultaneously to the future. Some prayers have been answered, some wait for their time to spring forth. Those faith sown prayers were invested in Jesus' never-ending Kingdom. They are still active, being answered. These are excellent investments! Every linear year of our lives we have the chance to make eternal investments. Ask Holy Spirit to show you how.

We get to experience the synergy of eternal investments made by others, including past generations. We can reap the rewards of family members and pioneers who paved trails of revival, those who paid a price to lay that road, so subsequent generations could walk on the firm ground of their sacrifice. "I am reminded of your sincere faith, which first lived in your grandmother Lois and in your mother Eunice and, I am persuaded, now lives in you also." (2 Timothy 1:5). Paul links Timothy's faith to the pioneering efforts of His grandmother who paved the way. She fought for faith in a family line and this came to Timothy via his mother Eunice. Abraham followed God as one of the first pioneers, paving the way of faith for us, "Therefore, the promise comes by faith, so that it may be by grace and may be guaranteed to all Abraham's offspring—not only to those who are of the law, but also to those who have the faith of Abraham. He is the father of us all." (Romans 4:16).

We need not reinvent the wheel, rather seek the inventions and treasures that the previous generations left for us. Utilize these and add our piece to pass to the next generations. We need eyes to see beyond now. Ask Holy Spirit to reveal anointings and gifts that are available to us and for the strategies to utilize them. Through unity and flourishing in our gifts, we synergize the redemptive power, becoming a Bride who unlocks a radiant future.

CHAPTER 14

Living within Limits; Interdependence that Achieves the Impossible

Paradoxically, we are vessels of God's power and we are limited. Partnered with Holy Spirit, we can do what is impossible for human beings yet God allows limitation to what we can accomplish on our own. Unity propels us beyond personal limitation, connecting us to the abundance of God. When my wife and I bought our house we acquired a line of invasive trees. Removing them has been a challenging process. One day I cut down one of the trees and hauled half of it into piles. This took me half a day. With the help of my wife and my neighbor we moved the remaining half and organized all the wood in only a couple of hours. Collaboration increased efficiency. This sparked a larger project, multiple neighbors contributed clearing the invasive trees and pruning good trees. Together we accomplished more and it cost each household less; we transformed a problem into an opportunity for new vision and beauty.

Transformation comes powerfully on both a personal and community level, with power to shift people, cities, and nations. Personal change fuels corporate transformation, but the community must actively choose changes. God willingly works with even a mustard seed size desire to change. Forced change, shifts circumstances but rarely changes the heart. Hearts must be affected to sustain transformation. Without buy-in, people begrudgingly comply with requirements, creating limited surface level change. When the enforcement lifts, transformation ends. God's goals are multifaceted and powerful, dependent on willing individual and corporate transformation. Great things await the individual, greater await the Bride, as she harnesses the power that comes from united transformation.

Jesus leads us into the outrageous prophetic call to, "rebuild the ancient ruins and restore the places long devastated; they will renew the ruined cities that have been devastated for generations." (Isaiah 61:4). This comes through the transformation of hearts. Multiple hearts transformed will renew ruined cities. It starts with transforming my heart, building deep connections with transformed lovers of God, awakening a culture of hope, restoring places long devastated. This requires authenticity, risk, and vulnerability. Willingly engaging tension and accounting for the possibility of getting hurt. This is the way of Jesus. The disciples modeled risk, leaving lives they understood to follow the Messiah. The early church risked sharing the gospel which sometimes resulted in prison, torture, or death. Jesus said, "Whoever wants to be my disciple must deny themselves and take up their cross daily and follow me." (John 9:23). Safety is not heaven's priority, transformation is, even if it costs my life.

Jesus invites us to a life of risk, called to an uncomfortable lifestyle beyond the world's vision of flourishing and success, instead instilling God's Kingdom that transforms the world. I believe that the Kingdom of God unleashed through the body of Christ, is the most powerful force of transformation in the world. In part, this is true because the Bride is full of those who have experienced authentic and life altering personal change. These united experiences catalyze results for others.

One way I've seen transformation in my life is through intentionally journaling and praying through my dreams. The discipline of getting myself out of bed in the early hours of the morning, writing while my eyes are half closed and brain a bit foggy, and later praying through what I've recorded has proved surprisingly fruitful. I have faithfully asked for and recorded dreams and developed a system that streamlines the key components of dreams. I've taken time to learn from people who have interpreted thousands of dreams and to learn God's unique dream language for me.

In June 2022, while writing this book, I had a dream that highlighted the incredible power of God's united Bride. I saw a trio of believers; they were passionate followers of Jesus, two women and one man. They came from different countries and at the outset of the dream, they had a somewhat awkward group interaction. They united to fix problems on the Golden Gate Bridge. They visited and noticed some serious structural issues and reported them. The bridge operator, in disgust and in an attempt to get rid of them, offered them keys and a small repair kit and said they could go up the bridge. It was a Sunday afternoon. To the operator's surprise they went. They walked up the huge cables, climbing to the tops of the towers. Their safety gear was minimal, helmets and a couple of short ropes, but nothing that would ensure safety if a disaster came. Their focus and resolve took them above fears, their trust was in Jesus. And strangely enough, they took a dog. They ascended together, depending on one another and championing their diverse and varied skills. These were skills that each had honed within. Though the bridge had been neglected, they fixed it. They redeemed what government authorities had irresponsibly failed to care for. Empowered by Holy Spirit, they did the impossible.

Unity that champions the gifts of each of us creates space for Holy Spirit to work impossible feats through us. Our fixed faith and dependency on Jesus lead the advance. The three people are a picture of the body of Christ, comprised of women and men and all ethnicities, ages, and socio-economic levels for His purposes. Unity comes only through beholding Jesus as our focal point, He connects us. This dream indicates that the body of Christ has authority and a mandate, to restore failed systems and structures. The secular government is an expression of power and order that does not inherently carry God's Kingdom authority. Jesus describes the church using the Greek word ekklesia, defined as God's legislative body on the earth. The church carries governmental authority to bring the truth of Heaven into the realm of the earth. Jesus says, "the gates of Hades will not overcome it. I will give you the keys of the kingdom of heaven; whatever you bind on earth will be bound in heaven, and whatever you loose on earth will be loosed in heaven." (Matthew 16:18-19). God imbues power to hold back and thwart the attack of evil. God is raising up His church to speak into government, as well as the marketplace, media, and every sphere of influence. He wants worldwide Kingdom order and alignment. The earth is God's. He is the God of breakthrough, the God of the impossible. He urges His united Bride to step with Him into those impossibilities and breakthroughs.

My friend Brian, read my dream and commented, "I think it might be prophetic of how the church will be taking over where the government fails. But the dog! The dog! They took a dog. This is a pet, which says it belonged to one of them. This pictured such a depth of confidence in the impossible God to do what they couldn't actually do! A dog on the cables??? That's a picture and a half. It's got to be significant." I think he's right. Bringing a dog on the mission signifies trust and faith permeating all levels of one's life, dependence on God who empowers us for the impossible. God calls us individually and collectively to take down giants, living in Jesus' victory, and embodying the incredible declaration, "Now to him who is able to do immeasurably more than all we ask or imagine, according to his power that is at work within us" (Ephesians 3:20). We need to increase our faith, vision, and trust so that God can accomplish all He desires through us. God seeks empowered lovers who follow Jesus' example, driving back the darkness and living out His prayerful mandate, "your kingdom come, your will be done, on earth as it is in heaven." (Matthew 6:10).

CHAPTER 15

Appreciate Variety;
Separate from Evil

Heaven comes to earth in power through the unity of the Bride. God desires the beauty that results as people with different perspectives, talents, and abilities connect. This comes with growing pains, tension, and wrestling with things we don't like or understand. God made us each unique, He knows the beauty of combining our differences, notwithstanding the challenges and accounting for the variety of preferences. God is glorified by the intricacy and beauty of the various parts. He loves the beauty in each of us. When all His kids are together, He sees the beautiful tapestry of His Bride. God's heart for His Bride requires that I dig to find the gold in others, even in the people that rub me wrong. This provides a framework to leverage the good for the benefit of all. To do this we have to look past obvious character issues, suspend judgment and silence accusations.

The prophetic is truly a gift of seeing the potential in

a person or a situation. This requires discernment, gaining God's vision of a person or situation. Then declaring the deeply embedded good, often calling out things that aren't apparent as though they are. This highlights the potential of what a person can access. Think of the prophet Ezekiel, who told dry bones to live again (Ezekiel 37:1-14). It's a story that has been turned into a light hearted Sunday school song. But imagine you stumbled upon an uncovered mass grave, not a morgue with bodies that were alive hours or days earlier. You are surrounded by skeletons, dried out by years in the sun. Skulls and bones with the flesh picked clean by scavengers; muscles, sinews, and organs long gone. The rational mind would assess these bones as lifeless shells of long dead people; without the faintest idea of anything else. God, however, reveals prophetic perspective through Ezekiel, unlocking insight from the spiritual realm and calling the natural realm to align. This empowered an army, not a couple corpses, but an army of skeletons, to live again. This is just plain weird, uncomfortable, and characteristically prophetic. Seeing and calling out the unfathomable, even what offends the natural mind. And this is why the prophetic gift is frequently misunderstood, even rejected. It is strange, hard to comprehend, and yet a gift God calls good.

The good things of God are often great mysteries, ones that need to be experienced more than logically comprehended. We have a propensity to avoid the irrational, uncomfortable, or things that cause pain. Pain experienced as we work with those different from us, frequently results in disengagement and failing to see the beauty available via collaboration. Jesus brought together opposites; fishermen and Pharisees, women and men,

Zealots and tax collectors. The modern equivalent would be Democrat and Republican, Baby Boomer and Millenial, soldier and pacifist. Our labels do not limit Jesus. He will commission those who hold opposing views for tasks requiring dependence on one another. We need each other, we need to lean into discomfort. Unity does not mean continual comfort, but rather yielding to the painful growth process that produces beauty and power. Learning to love and care for people that we struggle with unveils the fullness of God. Stay the course, love well, and hold space for all.

Jesus will bring people into your life that you do not agree with, particularly like, or want to be around. He will also bring those who we feel awkward around and have difficulty connecting with. That's okay, stay the course, show up, and attempt a relationship by allowing Holy Spirit to guide you. Choose to love every person that God puts in your path. Jesus' Bride has great breadth and depth, though easy to build rapport with those similar to us, we gain a necessary depth and spectrum of perspective through reaching across the aisle of difference. To see God's purpose come to fruition we must reach across the aisle.

Discerning Friend from Foe

Following Jesus means sharing His love with everyone. Love those who are for us and those who betray us. Not all who are Christians or attend church follow Jesus. "Watch out for false prophets. They come to you in sheep's clothing, but inwardly they are ferocious wolves." (Matthew 7:15).

Jesus wants us to be aware that wolves are lurking around the people of God, intent on our destruction. Be vigilant to discern friend from foe, and ask Holy Spirit for strategies in each situation.

Unity relies upon genuine intimacy. Intimacy with Jesus comes by surrendering all that distances us from Him. Attempting to foster evil practices and cultivate a relationship with Jesus inhibits the authentic fruit of unity. Paul mentions some of these inhibitors,

> *"The acts of the flesh are obvious: sexual immorality, impurity and debauchery; idolatry and witchcraft; hatred, discord, jealousy, fits of rage, selfish ambition, dissensions, factions and envy; drunkenness, orgies, and the like. I warn you, as I did before, that those who live like this will not inherit the kingdom of God." (Galatians 5:19-21)*

Sexual immorality, debauchery, orgies, and witchcraft are overt oppositions to God's Kingdom. But the subtle attitudes and issues of factions, envy, dissension, and jealousy are found in churches and frequently tolerated. God's holiness requires that we root out all sin.

> *"Very truly I tell you, unless a kernel of wheat falls to the ground and dies, it remains only a single seed. But if it dies, it produces many seeds. Anyone who loves their life will lose it, while anyone who hates their life in this world will keep it for eternal life." (John 12:24-25)*

Jesus highlights that following Him means yielding every part of our life, dying to unleash His Kingdom. An accurate assessment of Western Christianity reveals many are enmeshed in evil lifestyles. The unity of God is inhibited when evil is allowed to have a heartbeat. Christ leads us in diligently rooting out sin, surrendering our broken and misguided perspectives to Him and receiving healing. We cannot be slack about this; God's beauty and majesty must be known. Too many Western Christians knowingly nurse evil habits, but are unwilling to fully surrender to the crucible for cleansing.

King David's prayer in Psalm 139:23-24 guides the genuine pursuit of purity, "Search me, God, and know my heart; test me and know my anxious thoughts. See if there is any offensive way in me, and lead me in the way everlasting.". Continual cleansing, pursuing purity, and righteousness are non-negotiables for the unity of the Bride. For the health of the Bride, we need to be aware of whether the sin patterns we see in ourselves and others are the willful refusal to submit to King Jesus, or a two step forward, one step back growth process. Jesus supports those working through sin but with transparency that there is no room for compromise.

Unity leads to a delicate dance that includes creating space for people, discerning a friend from foe, embracing discomfort, and being open to learning new facets of God. I enjoy more of Jesus when I am able to engage with the fullness of all His children. I honor Jesus in others even when it's not my style or preference. Being open to a variety of expressions looks like a willingness to find Jesus in everything from the liturgical to charismatic expressions. It looks like sourcing discomfort and determining whether it is a dislike due to personal preference, something you haven't experienced of God, or because it isn't God. A friend remarked that she didn't want to miss out on something God is doing due to discomfort or inexperience. Holy

Spirit loves when we desire Jesus, and humbly lean in with a childlike posture.

Willingly appreciating the beauty of varied expressions allows me to experience God's fullness. Creating space requires being discerning, identifying truths and lies, and standing in truth. Discerning when someone is walking in a facet of God's truth that we haven't known, provides an opportunity to grow in our knowledge and experience of Jesus. Discerning when someone is walking in a lie, even with a sincere though misguided conviction, provides an opportunity to extend mercy.

The Bride has to guard against and refuse partnership with lies people are propagating. Seek the truth and hold to it, be gracious and loving when disagreeing. Don't partner or create space for ideas that are culturally acceptable but biblically heretical. Partnering with a lie that makes people feel good dishonors Christ. This is not unity, this is the breeding grounds of heresy. The Bible encourages standing firm in faith (Isaiah 7:9), and that we "resist the devil" (James 4:7). This can look like graciously calling out perspectives that are not biblical. This leads to unity. If a Christian willingly continues in a misguided conviction even after being presented with truth, distance is necessary. To keep a relationship with one openly embracing sin, enables sin without the consequences necessary to turn a heart. Cutting off the connection can awaken a person to truth. Sin and evil are not to be tolerated. Light and darkness cannot exist in the same space. Bow to Jesus and not to what feels right, is socially accepted, or seems "fair" to us. Unity comes in full submission to King Jesus.

CHAPTER 16

Maturity to Engage Conflict with Love

Jesus develops breadth and depth, smooths out our sharp edges, and trains us to dispense greater measures of grace through the people He brings into our lives. Conflict becomes a training ground, a growth opportunity, and provides potential to add depth to relationships as a redemptive tool for our growth. Conflict is tricky, easily becomes emotional, as feelings get hurt, and defensive mechanisms flare. Conflict engaged with love and honor allows relationships to stay intact and fruitful, guiding our responses away from divisive and accusatory spirits that desire to pounce when emotions rage. In the midst of conflict, prioritize connection, and seek to harness the power of conflict to refine and build. Conflict occurs throughout our lives, many go silent or become argumentative when encountering it, both are ineffective, we need to be equipped for it. Tact and grace help us walk through disagreement. Tact guides clarity in what you want to convey, grace leads us to share with humility. Trust and relational rapport allow us to speak deeply into another's life producing more effective outcomes.

Jesus had conflict with the breadth of people He interacted with, from the Pharisees to the disciples. The Pharisees lived under strict legalism and repeatedly tried trapping Jesus by asking complex questions. Jesus gained very little rapport with the Pharisees, except for the few who became His covert followers. Most remained fixed in their stifling legalism. In contrast, the disciples who spent a tremendous amount of time with Jesus, went through incredible trials. All but one took His corrective message to heart, spread it and changed the world. Conflict handled well unlocks transformational power.

Some gifts in the body of Christ are naturally conflict oriented. The prophetic, for example, introduces tension and creates conflict through presenting God's perspectives, which requires the listener to accept or reject them. Contrasted with those operating with the gift of helping, who are much less likely to stir up conflict. God creates space for conflict, desiring the difference and beauty that comes through the variety of gifts.

When God gives something difficult to share, the tone shared with helps the effectiveness of a corrective message. In 2 Samuel 12, the prophet Nathan tactfully brings to David's attention his sin of murdering Uriah and taking Bathsheeba as his wife. The tone he conveyed the message in allowed God to convict David. Contrasted to Matthew 14:1-12, where John the Baptist boldly proclaims to King Herod that it is unlawful for him to have Herodias as his wife. Herod imprisoned John and later beheaded him. At times, God will give us messages that may upset people.

The gospel will disrupt our ways that are not aligned with God, aiming to bring them into truth. The tone we communicate a message in can help produce a positive impact. The gospel confronts lies and forces all who hear to choose truth or lie. Sometimes God needs you to speak, even if it comes out awkward and messy. Examine your heart and listen for God's leading, making sure you are sharing with the hopes of seeing another flourish.

Conflict can also result from addressing an area of our weakness. We need help from the body of Christ to mature. Our growth comes both through God bringing people into our lives to aid maturity and through self-motivated steps of growth. A supple heart hungering for Jesus creates more opportunity for both. Though we need correction, I believe a healthy ratio is to frequently speak encouragement and occasionally with admonishment. Loving admonishment has its place, but we thrive on encouragement. Positive reinforcement has life-changing power. Our time in history is ripe with disapproval, normalizing and even celebrating criticism. A viable antidote is ramping up our encouragement.

Criticism and admonishment are vastly different. Criticism seeks to tear a person down. Admonishment gives timely, even passionate advice and encouragement in attempts to correct a misaligned way in order for another to flourish. Criticism often comes laced with hate, bullying, and pride. Admonishment is humble, imparting grace, wanting a person's success. Western culture is inundated with criticism but contains few examples of healthy admonishment. Holy Spirit wants to teach us this way that encourages, corrects with great love, and desires His people to grow into fullness.

Hyper sensitive or hyper emotional atmospheres can easily turn argumentative and critical; great tact and dependence on Holy Spirit allow for positive and constructive conversations in these contexts. Grace helps tense conversation prove fruitful. Indicators of a healthy relationship include pursuing connection and communicating with grace in the midst of disagreement. Grace holds strong boundaries, intervenes to confront unhealthy behavior, and defends the weak, marginalized, and voiceless. Grace does not avoid tension or intensity. Jesus often challenged the Pharisees with grace and love, He intentionally engaged tensions. "Woe to you, teachers of the law and Pharisees, you hypocrites! You shut the door of the kingdom of heaven in people's faces. You yourselves do not enter, nor will you let those enter who are trying to." (Matthew 23:13). Jesus admonishes the Pharisees for purposely blocking access to God, highlighting their call to lead people to Him and their active rebellion. With intensity and grace Jesus raises awareness and extends an invitation to repent.

Sometimes conversations miss the textbook protocols, we say things poorly, but nonetheless address them. God can still use this for the good of all involved. Grace helps these situations, yet doesn't provide us license to blunder conversations. We need to improve the ways that we convey God's heart. God invites us to try our best, make mistakes, learn, have a humble growth mindset, and to be quick to repent and seek opportunities to mature. God doesn't expect perfection. He wants our growth and provides grace for rough processes. God willingly redeems messes from our attempts to grow.

God's Kingdom came through both Solomon and

David. Solomon was a man of peace, who built a prosperous Israel that David won back by war. God's Kingdom comes through peaceful and confrontive actions, change can be catalyzed through peaceful building efforts or even by directly opposing evil. Rely on Holy Spirit for which tool to employ for your specific season. Sometimes watering the crops you want prevents the weeds from spreading. Other times it is necessary to uproot weeds in order for the good crop to flourish. Give attention to what matters, stay in step with Holy Spirit. Sometimes choosing not to address the weeds in another's life but instead being present and loving them will shift the situation. We carry catalyzing power in our being that impacts atmospheres, words are not always necessary, simply being present can influence change.

In our time, the atmosphere is volatile with potential for tension to explode in a moment. Demonic spirits seek to shipwreck relationships, luring us to partner with them by what we say. Our words have incredible power. "The tongue has the power of life and death, and those who love it will eat its fruit." (Proverbs 18:21). Our words impact the world; they are spiritually charged. Be diligent to speak life-giving words that unite and build up the Bride. "The soothing tongue is a tree of life, but a perverse tongue crushes the spirit." (Proverbs 15:4). Be a tree of life, speak truth, be willing to lay down being right, and learn to do conflict well, this is a healthy part of meaningful relationships.

When conversations turn volatile, we especially need to prioritize love, looking for creative ways to honor and willingly choose to avoid difficult topics. Choosing to prove why you are 'right' rarely results in relational rapport, instead love is lost. "Above all, love each other deeply, because love covers over a multitude of sins." (1 Peter 4:8). Loving well leads us to limit what we share, accounting for the depth a relationship can handle, and protecting our connection. Love leads us to agree to disagree, limit interactions, and take space for a season to preserve connection. Love leads us to change how we interact with another, and through prayer seeks God to bless and mold the relationship. Give God space to guide you to love with flexibility and creativity.

The word love means a variety of ideas depending on context. We need an accurate definition of love. Love is Jesus Christ ripped to shreds by whips, beard pulled out, spat on, mocked, unrecognizable. He is pierced with a crown of thorns, blood running down His body, hanging on a cross in agony, dying. His torturous death march is His proposal to His Bride. He had each of us in mind through the entirety of the horror He endured. Love is Jesus, the self-giving Savior, being wronged to ensure the benefit and redemption of all people. He paid the just price for an uncommitted sin and yet shouldered it as His own.

> *"Whoever does not love does not know God, because God is love. This is how God showed his love among us: He sent his one and only Son into the world that we might live through him. This is love: not that we loved God, but that he loved us and sent his Son as an atoning sacrifice for our sins." (1 John 4:8-10)*

Love is Jesus, the God of the universe, leaving perfection, becoming human, and dying for us, restoring the way to eternal relationship with God.

God's love is other oriented, benefiting His creation. Holy Spirit desires to empower us in the same self-giving life that Jesus modeled. Being self-giving is not the same as tolerating another. Being able to spend time with others, being civil and in the same room, yet harboring bitterness toward them is unhealthy, does not honor Jesus, and is not love. Jesus prioritizes reconciliation prior to worship, "Therefore, if you are offering your gift at the altar and there remember that your brother or sister has something against you, leave your gift there in front of the altar. First go and be reconciled to them; then come and offer your gift." (Matthew 5:23-24). Bitterness will destroy a heart. It is like acid that eats away from within. We have to heal and reconcile; this is foundational to the Christian life.

Tolerance chooses to hold distance and disdain and avoid contact with those disliked; minimal contact can normalize bitterness toward others, but the pure heart is clear of all bitterness. The longer the distance, bitterness, or disdain lasts, the more detrimental the results are in our lives, especially in our closest relationship. Either we address and heal from it or we continually build taller and thicker walls of denial and avoidance.

God championed us in our most broken and vile moment. Holy Spirit leads us to be champions for others. Love leads us to work through awkward and uncomfortable scenarios, surrender bitterness, and extend love. Love leads us to speak positive and encouraging words and shut our mouths when we have nothing good to say. This is a disciplined spiritual act of love that we need to encourage in one another and celebrate when we do. Let us become those who build with encouragement, engage conflict with love, and gently admonish, calling out the beauty and vision of King Jesus in our sisters and brothers.

CHAPTER 17

Honoring Differences

I received my master's degree from an ecumenical seminary with more than thirty different Christian denominations represented. We ranged from Episcopal to Pentecostal, practicing orderly liturgy to charismatic tongues. During that time we experienced one of the harshest American presidential elections in recent history. Our community had polarizing beliefs on all matters, and was not free from human drama. The tension was palpable, disconnect was in the air, and the atmosphere felt prone to volatility.

Through a series of events I ended up creating a monthly gathering for staff and students called *Depolarize*. It was a forum for us to share differing perspectives, learn about one another and seek Jesus. We focused on appreciating the beauty of God in our varied experience and expression of walking with Christ.

Intentionally creating space to grow in understanding unfamiliar perspectives and leaning into different ways is quite effective for connection. In our community these efforts helped us discover things we agreed on, develop rapport, and establish context to examine areas of difference with grace. This allowed us to diffuse some of the atmospheric tension, see one another, and access the love of God. Love allowed us to venture into the 'why?' behind our varied beliefs and practices, and this increased respect for the unique stories behind our perspectives. Love-based connection provided space for hope and depth of relationship.

All too frequently, people are willing to use a battering ram to break perceived wrong beliefs. A healthy alternative is to hold the tension, learn about different perspectives, and establish solid relational rapport before discussing tense questions. In recent years we have been trained and encouraged to attack the things we disagree with, prioritizing ideals instead of people. Media and social norms encourage attacking others for perspectives we deem unacceptable. Jesus leads us to love and live with tension, maintaining relationships, and mercifully accepting others as we find them. If we forgo developing relational rapport, we lose grounds for healthy conversation about emotionally charged perspectives. Our enemy wants us to believe that what we believe matters more than the person who holds the belief. Jesus' blood bought people, not perspectives. Perspectives are worth fighting for, but not at the cost of people. "Follow God's example, therefore, as dearly loved children and walk in the way of love, just as Christ loved us and gave himself up for us as a fragrant offering and sacrifice to God." (Ephesians 5:1-2).

The way of love is intentional, sometimes requiring that we choose to talk about areas of disagreement. Loving well requires addressing areas where God has provided a clear standard and others are holding a lie. We are called to bear the truth and guide people into all truth. Love correctly expressed will guide, even prophetically challenge one another, into truth.

"For God did not appoint us to suffer wrath but to receive salvation through our Lord Jesus Christ. He died for us so that, whether we are awake or asleep, we may live together with him. Therefore encourage one another and build each other up, just as in fact you are doing." (1 Thessalonians 5:9-11)

Conflict can be an effective means for building. Jesus gathered a diverse group of people around him, those who disagreed and struggled to see each other's point of view. Those who would rather not be together. Working through differences is a key part of this journey because we all see only in part. "For now we see only a reflection as in a mirror; then we shall see face to face. Now I know in part; then I shall know fully, even as I am fully known." (1 Corinthians 13:12). God alone sees the whole picture and distributes bits of truth to each of us. Collectively we represent the fullness, individually we represent a portion.

Marriage is a poignant example of individuals uniting for fullness. Couples work through tensions of different perspectives and ways, strength comes through the process. Spouses get stressed out trying to understand differences, not because they are wrong, rather they are not intuitive. Spouses have to create order that causes both to flourish through respecting and understanding differences in order to play to collective strengths. My wife and I benefit each other with our differences. I am good in rapid response, intuitive, and reactionary situations. She is excellent at developing structures and systems that become rhythms we live by. Our differences are a collective benefit, rather than a problem to be sorted. Healthy perspective is essential; an outlook that interprets challenges and differences as available opportunities, rather than painstaking problems, provides the foundation for flourishing.

One autumn, we traveled to Germany with my in-laws. We spent our first week in a village harvesting grapes for wine, then we took a train to a village on the Rhine river. The night before we left the Rhine, in the midst of a planning session, I had an epiphany. Our trip would be less stressful if we could quickly pivot from traveling by public transportation to renting a car. I proposed the idea that we pick up a car when we arrived in Frankfurt the next day. Though overwhelming in the moment, my wife understood my vision, leaned on my strength and applied her own, quickly comparing rental companies and securing a car that met our needs. The next day we picked up the car which indeed made the remainder of the trip more enjoyable for us.

Honoring and understanding our different experiences is also vital. God desires that we receive from the full expression and variety of the body of Christ. Appreciating the stories we have lived and honoring what we have to offer one another helps us to gain all that God wants for our lives, both individually and collectively. Extending kindness and being gracious peacemakers unlocks those stories. Offering hope and mercy, and believing in breakthroughs in our areas of need and misunderstanding allows for our gain.

When experiencing hurt, I must work all the harder to create a positive connection with another. Obviously, we don't get to control the state of the relationship but we do get to control our heart posture and how we will engage with another. I can continue offering love and positivity, wanting their best, even if I'm rejected. Positive connection might require hunting for an appropriate depth that the relationship can sustain, perhaps relating at a more superficial level. This helps to avoid areas of pain, building rapport and giving one another time to work toward healing. This creates the foundation for deeper levels of relationship in the future.

When hitting an impasse, it may be necessary to suspend or change the way you interact while increasing prayer for breakthrough. Speak blessing, forgive hurts, and trust God to redeem relationships as you contend in prayer. Hope does not disappoint,

> *"but we also celebrate in our tribulations, knowing*
> *that tribulation brings about perseverance; and*
> *perseverance, proven character; and proven character,*
> *hope; and hope does not disappoint, because the*
> *love of God has been poured out within our hearts*
> *through the Holy Spirit who was given to us."*
> *(Romans 5:3-5)*

This is what unity, love, and contending for someone looks like. The circumstances don't have to dictate the scenario that we choose to live out. I can actively pursue the abundance of God for someone through prayer and trust that even disconnected seasons will work for God's good. This is waiting with expectant hope. And this is a love that appreciates and sees the beauty in people within the complexity of life. God's way is actively honoring, caring, and pursuing blessings for others, even when relationships are distanced or paused.

CHAPTER 18

Humility and Pruning: Means of Alignment

We all go through difficult seasons, even those where we choose to pause or redefine relationships to preserve health. Refining our hearts in the fire of God's love, preserves the bonds of unity. Willingly following God into crucible moments, even seasons, burns impurities away, making us more like Jesus. This means positioning ourselves to receive God's correction. "One word of correction breaks open a teachable heart, but a fool can be corrected a hundred times and still not know what hit him." (Proverbs 17:10 TPT). The teachable learn when corrected, but the fool repeatedly endures the pain, never changing.

Refining is positive, it is the crucible, where God moves us from glory to glory. "And we all, who with unveiled faces contemplate the Lord's glory, are being transformed into his image with ever-increasing glory, which comes from the Lord, who is the Spirit." (2 Corinthians 3:18). A teachable heart is the precious avenue of ever-increasing glory. God opposes and humbles the proud. Pharaoh's prideful resistance of God led to his destruction, when God freed Israel from Egypt. "Pride goes before destruction, a haughty spirit before a fall." (Proverbs 16:18). God urges us to humble ourselves and receive life. "Humble yourselves before the Lord, and he will lift you up." (James 4:10). Humility is the nature of God which allows us to access our profound callings. Humility fuels unity, aligning us through our submission to God's reign. Choosing to let go of our priorities and align with God's brings about transformative beauty.

Unity and alignment are interconnected. The Bride of Christ will be in complete alignment with Jesus at the culmination of His return.

> "I saw the Holy City, the new Jerusalem, coming down out of heaven from God, prepared as a bride beautifully dressed for her husband. And I heard a loud voice from the throne saying, 'Look! God's dwelling place is now among the people, and he will dwell with them. They will be his people, and God himself will be with them and be their God. 'He will wipe every tear from their eyes. There will be no more death' or mourning or crying or pain, for the old order of things has passed away." (Revelation 21:2-4)

Until then, God refines and aligns His Bride, through trial and crucible.

God extends a free choice to partner with or reject Him in this process. Rejecting Him is separating from His body, like a limb struck with gangrene, corrupting the part until eventually it must be severed to prevent further destruction. If we quit receiving life from the vine we fail to be fruitful. God will not tolerate fruitlessness, either He will prune us to resurrect life or cut off and burn lifeless limbs. Humility results in pruning and greater fruit.

We need to remove ourselves from the lifeless, the prideful. "Do not be misled, 'Bad company corrupts good character.' Come back to your senses as you ought, and stop sinning." (1 Corinthians 15:33-34). Rejecting God's refinement process is willful misalignment. We make few, if any, neutral actions in life. We are either building God's Kingdom or tearing it apart. We live in a war with no fences to ride. Jesus says:

> *"Remain in me, as I also remain in you. No branch can bear fruit by itself; it must remain in the vine. Neither can you bear fruit unless you remain in me. I am the vine; you are the branches. If you remain in me and I in you, you will bear much fruit; apart from me you can do nothing. If you do not remain in me, you are like a branch that is thrown away and withers; such branches are picked up, thrown into the fire and burned." (John 15:4-6)*

Our daily hunger for truth and pursuit of Jesus produces Kingdom fruit.

Humility Motivates Growth

Each of us stewards truths from God, some we have mastered, others we are growing in. Humility acknowledges our process and seeks others to grow from what they have fought to possess. Some, through their acts of service, reveal Jesus. Others through hospitality, draw people into God's love. Some have tremendous experience with worship or prophecy. Honor the investment of those who have honed a gift and learn from them. The Bride benefits from all of God's gifts, they are necessary for His mission.

> *"So Christ himself gave the apostles, the prophets, the evangelists, the pastors and teachers, to equip his people for works of service, so that the body of Christ may be built up until we all reach unity in the faith and in the knowledge of the Son of God and become mature, attaining to the whole measure of the fullness of Christ... From him the whole body, joined and held together by every supporting ligament, grows and builds itself up in love, as each part does its work." (Ephesians 4:11-13, 16)*

Humility creates space to connect deeply even as we move at different paces. Emphasize shared areas of belief where we can amplify our unity. Building on what we hold in common, deepens our trust. Trust provides a solid foundation for loving forays to discuss areas of difference. Establishing trust reduces heightened emotions of differing viewpoints. When living in Ukraine it was difficult to build friendships but God overcame the barriers and gave me a friend, Sasha. I was American, he was Ukrainian; I was in my 20s, he was in his 40s; I met Jesus as a child, he met Jesus in his 30s, in prison; just to name a few differences. Yet we built our friendship through prayer, talking about Jesus, and Sasha taught me songs in Russian so we could play guitar and worship together. These were precious and holy times. By emphasizing our common love for Jesus and worship, we created depth, trust, and built a meaningful friendship. Though it was challenging to navigate language, culture, and spiritual differences, the tension made it more rewarding.

Be quick to find places of agreement and quick to avoid conflict that only leads to dissension. Paul lists a nasty category of sins in Romans 13:13 with dissension landing in the middle of it. Initially it seems like it doesn't belong, but the heart of dissension is pride. Paul writes "Let us behave decently, as in the daytime, not in carousing and drunkenness, not in sexual immorality and debauchery, not in dissension and jealousy.". Conflict, if not entered into with humility and grace, can easily spiral into dissension. So be careful in tense conversations and if you go astray, repent.

Repentance is a lifeline for the humble, essential for unity. Repentance is the willingness to admit being wrong, then doing whatever it takes to align with the truth. Repentance requires admitting guilt. In a culture that demands perfection, being wrong is a glaring disaster and freely owning a mistake can be relational suicide. Christ leads us in the freedom of being transparent, humble, and receiving His merciful correction. I cease trying to self-preserve through defending my efforts and ego. Instead I recognize that apart from partnership with Jesus, I can offer nothing of value. This frees me to submit, partnering with

His purposes. I yield to a greater King and a greater way. Giving up idols, including ego and being right, instead worshiping the true King. When I clearly understand the freedom gained through repentance, then preserving my status doesn't matter, I can admit my guilt, because all that matters is Jesus and His Kingdom. David expresses this beauty,

> *"Be exalted, O God, above the heavens; let your glory be over all the earth. ... I will praise you, Lord, among the nations; I will sing of you among the peoples. For great is your love, reaching to the heavens; your faithfulness reaches to the skies. Be exalted, O God, above the heavens; let your glory be over all the earth." (Psalm 57:5, 9-11)*

Repentance restores me to my rightful place of singing the glory of God among God's people.

Humility builds the desire for what Jesus wants, He is returning for a glorious, united Bride. Understanding all that Jesus is doing is not prerequisite to embracing it as best as we know how. Consider our complex physical bodies. The various systems, digestive, nervous, muscular and others are incredibly detailed. I don't understand the intricacies of what takes place in each. I know some aspects of what is helpful. And there are systems in the body that I don't have the remotest understanding of; I simply trust them to perform their functions.

The body of Christ is a complexity of intricately detailed systems. I will not understand all the parts. God is ever increasing and longs to reveal mysteries to us that we don't have a framework for. Being humble, open-hearted, and teachable allows God to reveal more of these mysteries, to shock and awe us. As finite beings we will never be able to grasp the fullness of God. He made each one of us unique and He is partnering with us in a myriad of ways. It is okay when we encounter gifts, people, even Christian movements that are difficult to understand. We can still choose to enter in with a discernment that is looking for God's goodness at work even when it is uncomfortable, unclear, or foreign. God is looking for a growth mindset and a willingness to embrace His glorious mystery.

Humility Fuels Hunger for God

God is looking for the hungry and humble. God uses messy people, like King David, who are hungry, with a heart after God, and humble themselves to be vessels for God to do mighty things. God uses humble vessels who are less messy, like Mary, who carried the God of the universe in her womb. God simply looks for the humble and willing. Those who set their own limitations of what they will allow God to do in them miss the mighty tasks because they've created their own ceilings. Often choosing creature comforts above the risks and challenges that come in the life of faith. God looks for those offering their whole selves as vessels, becoming conduits of His full love. Those willing to come without terms get the most from God because they offer the greatest levels of trust. Fear drives self-protection, rejecting what is uncomfortable. Self-preservation and defensive tactics can be a result of trauma and even comes from a subconscious level. Identifying the roots of our responses takes us into the healing work with Jesus that results in greater trust.

Jesus calls us not according to who we are currently, rather to become what He sees and empowers us to be. Though God uses those who are outwardly put together, Jesus has a history of using the weak things of the world to confound the strong. "But God chose the foolish things of the world to shame the wise; God chose the weak things of the world to shame the strong." (1 Corinthians 1:27). God uses us in every stage of our journey, He is the great economizer. Jesus can use us at various points in our maturity because we are seated in heavenly places with Christ. A part of us is already with Him in glory. He is willing to pour into the brokenness of where we may be today to yield and bring about the fullness He knows will take place in eternity. "And God raised us up with Christ and seated us with him in the heavenly realms in Christ Jesus, in order that in the coming ages he might show the incomparable riches of his grace, expressed in his kindness to us in Christ Jesus." (Ephesians 2:6-7). God is not held back by us, in fact, He wants to do greater redemptive works in and through us than we can grasp.

God shines His redemptive beauty even in the completely broken person who He cleans up and empowers for His purposes. John Newton, who wrote the hymn, *Amazing Grace*, is a great example of this. God saved him from the brokenness of slave trading, immorality, and drunkenness. He equipped Newton to be a pastor. His former sins did not prevent God from using him mightily. Many are born with gifts that rest dormant through seasons of sin but salvation sprouts seeds that bear the fruit of God's Kingdom.

God loves to transform and bring glory to Himself, especially through audacious stories like the Apostle Paul.

Prior to Paul's incredible transformation, he lived an outwardly justified life. In his zealous legalism, he didn't experience God's love. Those chained to spirits of legalism and religion walk the narrow road, but with calloused self-righteousness on the surface of their hearts. They have lost pliability in their attempts to justify themselves. They carry titles, experiences, outward justifications; they are accomplished by the world's standards, but their hearts are distant from God. But God knows how to use a trial to unite us to Him and draw out the gold within. "In the same way that gold and silver are refined by fire, the Lord purifies your heart by the tests and trials of life." (Proverbs 17:3 TPT).

When those who attempt their own justification through their accolades have a life-transforming trial, their accolades, good works, and positions of authority become strengths and benefits to the Kingdom of God. God utilizes the things we treasured and attempted to justify ourselves with, rightfully connecting these with His Kingdom purposes. In Paul's case, his justifications included being,

> *"circumcised on the eighth day, of the people*
> *of Israel, of the tribe of Benjamin, a Hebrew of*
> *Hebrews; in regard to the law, a Pharisee; as for*
> *zeal, persecuting the church; as for righteousness*
> *based on the law, faultless. But whatever were gains*
> *to me I now consider loss for the sake of Christ.*
> *What is more, I consider everything a loss because*
> *of the surpassing worth of knowing Christ Jesus my*
> *Lord, for whose sake I have lost all things. I consider*
> *them garbage, that I may gain Christ and be found*
> *in him, not having a righteousness of my own that*
> *comes from the law, but that which is through faith*

in Christ—the righteousness that comes from God
on the basis of faith." (Philippians 3:5-9)

Under the blood of Christ, Paul's accolades no longer justified him, instead they became tools to build God's Kingdom. Jesus wants to turn all of us into influential firebrands, redeeming our stories for Kingdom impact.

Humility That Gives All

We exist to magnify God; we were made to worship. God is looking for people who will lay everything down for Him. People who don't need a variety of things in place can be greatly used in the Kingdom. There is even meaning to be had in suffering with Christ. "I want to know Christ—yes, to know the power of his resurrection and participation in his sufferings, becoming like him in his death, and so, somehow, attaining to the resurrection from the dead." (Philippians 3:10-11). Even martyrdom brings Jesus glory, a martyr unites with Christ's death on the cross.

In the garden of Gethsemane, Jesus models surrendering our preferences, showing humble submission to the Father. "'Father, if you are willing, take this cup from me; yet not my will, but yours be done.' An angel from heaven appeared to him and strengthened him. And being in anguish, he prayed more earnestly, and his sweat was like drops of blood falling to the ground." (Luke 22:42-44). This is full trust in God's plan, humble partnership, enduring an immense trial, releasing overwhelming beauty.

Submission to God, through living out the step of

faith, can result in separation from those around me. Shortly after Jesus prayed with blood-soaked tears, all His followers deserted Him. Yet God sent angels to strengthen Him. Hold to God, He promises to be with us no matter what we go through. Faith comes with resistance, sometimes severe opposition, this can affirm being in the center of God's beckoning. Watch for the log jam of legalistic wrestling over every idea based on the feelings and reactions that come from it. We can get bogged down by trying to make sure we haven't missed something. He wants us to develop a childlike trust that we are secure in His good plan. Even amidst tension, the pain we experience, brings Jesus glory. Trust God to bring beauty through pain and willingly lay down your life to live that story.

Following Jesus requires giving our entire hearts for His redemptive story. Jesus embraces you where you are, but to follow Him, you can't remain as you are. Refusing to relinquish all areas of your heart is rebellion. Warped and lukewarm theology presents a controllable Jesus, neglecting His self-sacrificing example. It is like a marriage where the couple is faithful, wearing rings, living together, raising kids faithful, yet lacks intimacy. No deep conversations, no desires and dreams, no romance. Is this a marriage? In some form certainly, but it's not the passionate picture of marriage between Jesus and His Bride.

> *"My lover said to me, 'Rise up, my darling! Come away with me, my fair one! Look, the winter is past, and the rains are over and gone. The flowers are springing up, the season of singing birds has come, and the cooing of turtledoves fills the air. The fig trees are forming young fruit, and the fragrant grapevines are blossoming. Rise up, my darling!*

*Come away with me, my fair one!"' (Song of
Songs 2:10-13 NLT)*

God motions us into the beautiful adventure He
created us for. Humility grasps this, willingly relinquishing
control, embracing the great adventure of love. Jesus wants
to give us more. The adventure gets better with time. We
get to advance further and deeper into His love and His
Kingdom which is breaking in with greater measure each
day. Those hungry for Jesus willingly lay down their lives,
repent quickly, and invest all in God's purposes. They
fight for the Bride rather than preserving themselves, hold
steadfast convictions, and continually offer love.

Dietrich Bonhoeffer lived this way. He saved Jews,
confronted the evils of the Nazi regime, and became a
martyr for Jesus. Perhaps had he given up his Christian
conviction he would have lived. Instead, he continually
offered love and compassion to his captors who represented
a violent, abusive, anti-Jesus system. He followed the
example of the Shepherd who gave His life for His sheep.

Humility Marked by Trust of God's Process and Sovereignty

The humble embrace the process of God, recognizing
the truth of His ways yield fruit. How we live matters as
much as what we produce. In God's Kingdom positive
outcomes come through healthy processes. God's processes
instill fruitful transformational truth. We must pray in order
to unlock the truth. Prayer is an essential weapon. Prayer
is a main weapon serving to reveal truth. Our prayers pave

the way for others to have dynamic encounters with Jesus, experiencing His love as incarnate truth. We cannot force people into truth, force will not produce the authentic fruit that Jesus desires. "I am the way and the truth and the life. No one comes to the Father except through me." (John 14:6). Jesus reveals truth as relational, it is not mastery of concepts, rather truth is a person, Jesus is truth.

Experiencing Jesus leads to seeking correction and embracing the pruning process that leads to life and unity. Pruning leads to personal transformation; giving us a means to offer compassion and grace to others. Surrendering to God's sovereignty and pruning actively abdicates the performance, approval, and competition race. Jesus modeled humility and surrender to God's sovereignty.

> *"Do nothing from selfishness or empty conceit [through factional motives, or strife], but with [an attitude of] humility [being neither arrogant nor self-righteous], regard others as more important than yourselves. Do not merely look out for your own personal interests, but also for the interests of others. Have this same attitude in yourselves which was in Christ Jesus [look to Him as your example in selfless humility], who, although He existed in the form and unchanging essence of God [as One with Him, possessing the fullness of all the divine attributes—the entire nature of deity], did not regard equality with God a thing to be grasped or asserted [as if He did not already possess it, or was afraid of losing it]; but emptied Himself [without renouncing or diminishing His deity, but only temporarily giving up the outward expression of divine equality and His rightful*

dignity] by assuming the form of a bond-servant, and being made in the likeness of men [He became completely human but was without sin, being fully God and fully man]. After He was found in [terms of His] outward appearance as a man [for a divinely-appointed time], He humbled Himself [still further] by becoming obedient [to the Father] to the point of death, even death on a cross. For this reason also [because He obeyed and so completely humbled Himself], God has highly exalted Him and bestowed on Him the name which is above every name, so that at the name of Jesus EVERY KNEE SHALL BOW [in submission], of those who are in heaven and on earth and under the earth, and that every tongue will confess and openly acknowledge that Jesus Christ is Lord (sovereign God), to the glory of God the Father." (Philippians 2:3-11 AMP)

The Son of God, yielded His life to the Father, humbling Himself and trusting God's Sovereign plan. Jesus supports us in the humble way of the Messiah, through humility and pruning we produce the glory of God.

CHAPTER 19

Hear God's Heart to Build His Kingdom

Listening indicates your value and care for another. The active choice of suspending one's beliefs, perspectives, and opinions in order to engage the perspective of another. Listening to Jesus leads to surrendering to His ways. Good things come when we submit to and honor God.

God is speaking. He wants us to hear Him, so listen expectantly. Sometimes He will lead you to address problems, requiring that you engage in conflict. Even when glaring evil takes place, choose to extend His grace, love, and peace. "Be merciful, just as your Father is merciful." (Luke 6:36). Extending mercy comes with a reward, "Blessed are the merciful, for they will be shown mercy." (Matthew 5:7). We never get to throw people away, not even an evil dictator, human trafficker, abuser, or person with an opposing perspective.

Jesus, with His unfathomable love, desires a relationship with every one of us. His willing self-sacrifice provided the freedom for us to choose this relationship. Jesus created all human beings with eternity in mind. He never wanted to be disconnected. Prioritizing connection with God and others requires working through areas of disconnect and misalignment. To partner with Jesus requires stoking the fires of hope, recognizing that no situation is beyond God's grace to redeem.

We will face incredibly difficult situations because we live in a spiritual war. God's redemptive love pursues those opposing Him. The unredeemed mind is hostile to God; the unsurrendered are by default against Jesus. James 4:4 asserts, "You adulterous people, don't you know that friendship with the world means enmity against God?". Admitting the spiritual battle we live in is the first step toward discovering the tools we need to face difficult differences. No matter how well-crafted and logical an argument, it will not break a spiritual hold. We need fiery prayers flowing with the power of Holy Spirit to break spiritual bonds. Our enemy actively works to get us wound up in logical arguments, like a dog chasing his tail, as we attempt to solve by reason, what can only be broken with spiritual tools. Some are captive to demonic thoughts, living chained to lies of the enemy, including Christians. We all are susceptible to the deceiver. The lies must be broken by the truth of scripture through the power of Holy Spirit's specific strategies to win spiritual battles.

Listen to God for the good in others and seek His ways of engaging brokenness with redemptive intent. Bring the correct tools and methods to the situations Jesus guides you to. Jesus reveals His greatest desire in John 6:39-40,

> *"And this is the will of him who sent me, that I shall lose none of all those he has given me, but*

raise them up at the last day. For my Father's will
is that everyone who looks to the Son and believes
in him shall have eternal life, and I will raise them
up at the last day."

We carry this truth into our interactions. We don't need to win arguments. We need to complete the mission of heaven, being conduits of God's love that all would become children of our Father, through Jesus our Savior.

As vessels of God's redemption we are going to face tensions, encounter difficulties and disagree. Holding space in the tension provides ways for God's love to come despite discomfort. God's Bride has struggled to model loving in the midst of disagreement and holding space for difference. Instead, impasses lead to splitting and failing to see opportunities for growth.

During college, I attended a weekly student outreach that included worship, teaching, and a meal. Hundreds of students came to powerful worship times, some of us joyfully danced. This became a tension. For months a group of us sat conspicuously in the first row of the sanctuary, but off to the side, where we had ample space to dance. Some of the leaders believed our dancing was distracting, we believed we were responding to God's presence.

Eventually the leaders asked us to move to the back of the sanctuary to dance, we complied, trusted God to meet us, but had a different experience, something tangible had been lost and we felt sadness. It seemed image and comfort took priority, failing to celebrate a generation who danced for God. This could have been handled better. We could have listened to God together, seeking His heart on the matter, building connection and honoring one another. It is easy to avoid conflict, but there is fullness of life available through conflict handled well. We attempted conflict resolution, continued attending, and still experienced God's goodness as He matured us and Jesus took great pleasure in our worship.

When difficulty occurs in our relationships, it is easy to shoulder it like we've done something wrong, but often we are simply experiencing the refining process. God puts us in relationships that shave away rough edges. That is neither an easy nor enjoyable process. Our enemy wants us to isolate, erecting walls of defense to preserve the safety we define. God is not looking for us to protect ourselves. He leads us to conflict and tension, perhaps through a boss, spouse, or child. This person refines us to bring Him greater glory. Do not fear tension or conflict. First, anchor yourself in your identity as a beloved child, then engage the conflict looking for the beauty available.

Jesus uses the crucible to purify us. We won't live our whole lives in it, but He leads us there to burn away impurity.

> *"He will sit as a refiner and purifier of silver;*
> *he will purify the Levites and refine them like*
> *gold and silver. Then the LORD will have men*
> *who will bring offerings in righteousness, and the*
> *offerings of Judah and Jerusalem will be acceptable*
> *to the LORD, as in days gone by, as in former*
> *years" (Malachi 3:3-4)*

God used the crucible to burn the evil out of the Levites, restoring them to bring beauty and righteousness. The crucible can be a consequence of sin but, "do not despise the chastening of the LORD, Nor detest His correction; For whom the LORD loves He corrects, Just as a father the son [in whom] he delights." (Proverbs 3:11-12 NKJV).

Refining aids us, seeing clearer, and becoming a benefit to others. God doesn't call us to judge, as in we are not to condemn or make a final say on a person's eternal status with God. That is God's role; He is the only one qualified. God, however, commissions us to hold lines and lead others in truth, and to speak honestly and prophetically against evils. Love honestly addresses evil, conveying that certain lifestyle choices, actions, and beliefs separate us from God. It is appropriate to stand against murder, abortion, sexual immorality, and greed, with love and not self-righteousness and condemnation. To promote sin increases pain, destruction, and rejects God. Jesus offers redemption to those who repent. He delights to extend mercy, compassion, and forgiveness. Often people say "Don't judge me, you're not God." This is an attempt to hide and avoid a confrontation with sin. God, however, commissioned His Bride to model the truth of His Kingdom and hold lines of His order. We have to share the messages of truth and the tone we transmit these messages in is of utmost importance. Sometimes less is more; be brief, clear, and kind.

Unity means honest and heartfelt conversations, cultivating this intimacy is necessary for greater movements of God. The unity of the Bride will be a channel for the global outpouring of God's Spirit. Our collective faith will release exponential breakthroughs beyond what we could envision, for an incredible harvest.

During Jesus' ministry, a non-Jewish woman met Jesus with faith that impressed Him.

> "A Canaanite woman from that vicinity came to him, crying out, 'Lord, Son of David, have mercy on me! My daughter is demon-possessed and suffering terribly.' Jesus did not answer a word.

So his disciples came to him and urged him, 'Send her away, for she keeps crying out after us.' He answered, 'I was sent only to the lost sheep of Israel.' The woman came and knelt before him. 'Lord, help me!' she said. He replied, 'It is not right to take the children's bread and toss it to the dogs.' 'Yes it is, Lord,' she said. 'Even the dogs eat the crumbs that fall from their master's table.' Then Jesus said to her, 'Woman, you have great faith! Your request is granted.' And her daughter was healed at that moment." (Matthew 15:22-28)

This woman accessed the power of God through her great faith. Her faith released a miracle to her daughter and the news of her healing caused multitudes of the afflicted to gather, Jesus healed them, changing lives. This woman's great faith catalyzed a revival in her region. Do not despise small beginnings or dismiss people who are seemingly in the wrong camp, like this Canaanite woman. It is God's will to draw all people into the Kingdom. Look for those with faith or ripe for a God encounter. Ask God for prayer strategies to reach those around you. God is building His Kingdom and has commissioned us as builders.

CHAPTER 20

Patience and Grace for Growth

Unity requires listening to God's heart, increasing our patience and grace for the growth process, and seeing the gifts in each other. We only see in part and limited perspective cannot grasp the full vision of God. Relationships need not be killed by difference and disagreement. Maintain grace for another's journey, even when the ugliness of a person sorting their brokenness is uncomfortable. Through grace and mercy we maintain connection, allowing us to support another in their process.

It is often cultural to avoid and shame people when ugly issues come to light. We are fixated on success, and increasingly encourage the condemnation and punishment of those who fail, especially morally. I'm not advocating for moral failure or abandoning excellence. Yet in the midst of failure we all need advocates who guide us back to the Good Shepherd and the true ways. Consequences are necessary for the choices we make, we have to live through the ramifications of those. But punishment and consequence are different. A consequence applies boundaries and protections while maintaining a person's freedom and empowers him to clean up his mess, encouraging maturity and redemption. Punishment binds a person, takes away freedom and forces the punished to live according to what the punisher determines. This does not support transformation, growth, and maturity. Punishment doesn't bring the transformation deep in a person's core necessary to produce fruit. Punishment often reinforces the hurts that produced the failure.

Isaiah prophesied that Messiah would take our punishment, "He was pierced for our transgressions, he was crushed for our iniquities; the punishment that brought us peace was on him, and by his wounds we are healed" (Isaiah 53:5). Jesus redeems sinners, often this happens when one is desperate, having hit rock bottom. These failures, almost without question, are rooted in deep seated lies from the accuser, that kill the identity and innocence of a person. These lies come out sideways when people face stressful times. Jesus can redeem any story, no matter how ugly or evil the actions. Sin and the effects of it still have to be cleaned up, but Jesus loves redeeming sinners. Jesus leads us into the tension of ugly situations in our lives and the lives of others, freely extending His grace that is able to beautifully redeem. Jesus purposely uses tension to refine groups of people. He unites opposites, Zealot and tax collector, prostitute and Pharisee, sinner and saint. He brings people of wildly different life experience, philosophy, and conviction together, desiring to bring a collective beauty from an intensity of expression. We cannot reject people, especially in the body of Christ, but it is appropriate to draw healthy boundaries, even choosing not to speak about certain subjects for a set amount of time. Boundaries preserve relationships, allowing for the pursuit of maturity, and gaining tools for deeper means to connect.

In order to reach greater alignment, we have to work through differences. We approach life from various outlooks. I cannot completely understand another's perspective, but I can connect deeply through learning more of another's view. It is helpful to gain insight about one another. Having a common target of where God is taking us will allow us to grow together and mature quickly as we pursue collective assignments from God. We can partner well with others in current and future projects without having to know a person's past. We need to avoid navel-gazing and camping out in the past, these will distract from the current and future motion God has for us. Fixing our gaze on Jesus, allows us to live into our redeemed identity, new creatures in Him, no longer what we were before Christ.

We live in a fast paced society. Our guide, Holy Spirit, knows how to unite people living at this tempo. He knows our unique stories of pain, joy, fullness, grace, mistakes, but He covers all these with His beauty.

"For what we preach is not ourselves, but Jesus Christ as Lord, and ourselves as your servants for Jesus' sake. For God, who said, 'Let light shine out of darkness,' made his light shine in our hearts to give us the light of the knowledge of God's glory displayed in the face of Christ. But we have this treasure in jars of clay to show that this all-surpassing power is from God and not from us." (2 Corinthians 4:5-7)

God chooses common jars of clay to host his beauty. Partner with God to unveil the beauty in yourself and others.

Jesus is reforming and filling a Bride with His beauty. As we encourage each other, we bolster the Bride's hope and transformation. We don't need to agree on all minor points before we can support one another. We will not avoid the problems, but we can work through them and recognize there are some issues that don't need our time. Some people take glory in their problems and share them in detail. They gain attention through a victim mindset, rather than pursuing healing, more of Jesus, or moving beyond the wound. God is a comforter and wants to sit with us in our pain, but always to redeem it and break the chains of hurt. God can handle all our brokenness, but people cannot. We must be careful not to pour on others what only God has capacity for. We need to direct others to God when they are pouring pain on us that He alone can heal. God connects with us in our pain and validates our hurts with the purpose of healing us. God loves to turn the pains and attacks of the enemy into springboards revealing His goodness and beauty.

God accepts us in the condition that we find ourselves in today. Deep, lasting change typically takes time but there are times where Jesus will transform a situation in a moment. I have a friend who was addicted to cocaine, but the night he surrendered to Jesus, the addiction ceased, his desire for cocaine instantaneously left and never returned. Though other areas of his growth and maturity required time and intentional effort.

Our consistency on the long road to lasting change encourages others through our example. Our ability to effectively minister starts with receiving that ministry for ourselves. The long road is God's beautiful path of our transformation. We discard default patterns that we've been stuck in our whole lives. This transformation can take years. I have met people who were entrenched in sin, addicted to drugs, sex, and other soul tearing bondages. Yet the moment they received Jesus, the shackles of their slavery broke, as they became free children of God. Others have to take up arms, do battle with the enemy, and fight the good fight of faith for full freedom. Often this is a process of changing behaviors and then attacking the core lies so that Christ's freedom reigns. God does redemptive work through all tempos of change. We find ourselves at various stages in our process. We need space and grace to walk out this journey. Our lives are an ongoing process of being transformed into Christ's image. This maturity journey will produce a greater harvest for Christ. As we make space for ourselves in the journey of change, we create grace for those around us to follow our example.

Though it is good to hope and pray for quick changes, I have to learn to accept longer processes, and even relish the slow and deep work. Jesus loves the journey! God is so good at guiding us from one place to the next. We need patience for the long process of sustainable change. This sustainable healing process can resemble sourdough bread rising (days), home brewed beer (weeks), or the growth of babies (months). We will lose integral components through rushing the process. It is necessary to do the long, slow, deep work of growth. We benefit by cultivating grace that encourages growth in ourselves and others. We need the grace of Jesus during this process. This is our way forward, this is the path of united maturity.

CHAPTER 21

Reconciliation and Repentance

The growth process comes with unavoidable blunders; these prove to be the building blocks of maturity. Growth is painful and sometimes includes severe consequences. Some choose not to grow because they want to avoid pain. We can take the path of the servant who buried his talent in Matthew 25, but his consequence was eternal condemnation. Safety in God's Kingdom is not avoiding pain. Safety is simply being with Jesus. With Him we endure the fires of refinement, trial, and persecution. With God our mistakes become opportunities for redemption that highlight God's beauty. Anticipate growing pains and be willing to ask Jesus for help cleaning up messes to redeem mistakes made. The alternative is walking the tightrope of performance, when we fail, the pain is immense, the way back grueling, and the cycle exhausting. We can encourage growth and maturity of the Bride through developing grace for ourselves and one another in our journey. God is gracious to us, receiving His grace allows us to extend that to others. We all need to grow and we all need grace.

Reconciliation is a fabric of the growth journey. We need to both offer and receive reconciliation. Some mistakes are rooted in deep sin and have painful, possibly life altering consequences. Identifying root causes behind missteps helps in the process of reconciling. Some blunders come in our growth process as we try things and fail. The learning process requires attempting a new thing, sometimes these efforts will go very poorly. Jesus creates space for our growth and responds with mercy to our errors, He teaches us to do the same for one another. He heals us in the reconciliation process and teaches us to be reconcilers. Paul exhorts Christians to be ministers of reconciliation.

"Christ's love controls us. Since we believe that Christ died for all, we also believe that we have all died to our old life. He died for everyone so that those who receive his new life will no longer live for themselves. Instead, they will live for Christ, who died and was raised for them. So we have stopped evaluating others from a human point of view. At one time we thought of Christ merely from a human point of view. How differently we know him now! This means that anyone who belongs to Christ has become a new person. The old life is gone; a new life has begun! And all of this is a gift from God, who brought us back to himself through Christ. And God has given us this task of reconciling people to him. For God was in Christ, reconciling the world to himself, no longer counting people's sins against them. And he gave us this wonderful message of reconciliation. So we are

*Christ's ambassadors; God is making his appeal
through us. We speak for Christ when we plead,
"Come back to God!" For God made Christ, who
never sinned, to be the offering for our sin, so that
we could be made right with God through Christ."
(2 Corinthians 5:14-21 NLT)*

We have all died in Christ. Good comes through partnering with Jesus in the new life. We cannot produce fruit on our own. Attempts to create good apart from Christ, creates a system of judgment and performance, doling out merit based on what each person produces. We all have equal access to Jesus, partnering with Him is the only way to yield fruit. It is not about how good we are, rather it's about how much we've humbled and yielded ourselves to Jesus. Being reconciled to Christ levels the playing field.

Mistakes can come when we are not aligned with Jesus. To be reconciled we need someone who will lovingly embrace and help us see how we've gone wrong and draw us back into alignment. Jesus doesn't hold our sin against us, He annuls it. We have to follow His example. When we make a mistake we need someone who can reconcile us to our Savior, someone who extends compassion, grace, and truth. This is an honor that Jesus calls all His followers into.

Alignment and reconciliation are multifaceted, with an overarching vision to move from death to life. God wants complete reconciliation and renewal in every part of our lives. Through Christ we are restored to favor with God. Though saved and saints, we still have broken areas to clean up. Those broken pieces don't get to speak the final word. Jesus declares that we are saved, loved, and redeemed. This reality begins when we surrender to Him, even though we still have messes in our life. We're called to advocate, guiding the body of Christ to live the reality of reconciliation.

Reconciliation requires repentance. Repentance is a humbling act of admitting where we were wrong. Sometimes it is black and white as in the case of stealing something. We admit the wrong, receive forgiveness, make restitution, and are made whole. It is really important to voice our sins, to own them, because this humility frees us from finding identity in our ability to perform. Our performance will never meet God's standard. Through voicing our failures, we admit our weakness and this allows Christ's blood to be our strength, speaking redemption into our lives. This doesn't mean letting go of standards or abandoning accountability. Rather this is how we develop the way of grace that reinstates us and others when we stumble. King David highlights God's faithfulness in reinstating the saint, "The LORD directs the steps of the godly. He delights in every detail of their lives. Though they stumble, they will never fall, for the LORD holds them by the hand." (Psalm 37:23-24 NLT). We are not Godly because we do everything right; we are Godly because we put our faith and trust in Jesus and He upholds us. We also take steps moving in directions as best we know how, stumbling, reconciling, but moving toward God's fullness.

In some situations reconciliation is not about admitting a sin of commission, willfully choosing sin, rather we need to recognize sins of omission. Sins of omission can be a little less obvious. They are stepping away from the favor of God, omitting to partner with God's good purpose for us. Often these are marked by loss and a sense of missing something, perhaps encountering a situation we did not know how to effectively handle.

Once I was hiking in the Chiricahua Mountains in Arizona with my wife. It was close to dusk and about half a mile from the trailhead we came upon a rattlesnake. Being from Portland, I'd never encountered a rattlesnake in the wild. When I heard the rattle, I responded with a deep-in-my-biology protective mode in ways that I never knew were in me. My body reacted so fast that my mind didn't have time to understand what happened. In a split second, I had a blueprint of the position of my wife, myself, and the rattlesnake. I instinctively knew the appropriate moves to make based on where the snake moved. Fortunately, the snake quickly slithered away.

Sometimes we encounter circumstances, conversations, or interactions that cause instinctive protective responses. Later, when reviewing what happened, we can make connections, understand what took place and become empowered to proceed in a healthy way. We all carry some level of unresolved issues and are bound to have these pockets of friction pop up from time to time. These are actually opportunities for healing and maturity.

A friend and I worked through some frictions in our relationship that came from our different beliefs, convictions, and experiences. The reconciliation came via a conversation I had with a pastor who knew enough about our disconnect to pose a few questions. Distance and loss, almost without question, are evidence of our enemy at play. The friction we faced broke some trust causing recoil, unsure if we had each other's best interest in mind. We were unsure whether we were united in our efforts, so we ran from the tension. We quit speaking for a year. As I chewed on the questions the pastor posed, Holy Spirit encouraged me to sort my feelings and thoughts into a letter. By faith with no strings attached I mailed it. It was an attempt to restore friendship. A few days later I received a text message thanking me for willingly leaning into friendship. We later met up for coffee, prayer, and restored our connection.

Reconciliation is a process of yielding to the whispers of God, trusting Him in the small and big actions He guides us to take. Sometimes willingly, other times reactionarily, we step away from something good because we don't have capacity to sort the pain that comes up. We choose not to engage the mystery to see what we could learn. The more years I walk with Jesus, the more mystery I see. I have experienced a plethora of mysteries of Jesus that I do not understand. My understanding is not necessary. I simply need to follow the Lamb wherever He goes. Willingness to extend mercy, love, and to desire the fullness of life help this pursuit. Following the Lamb often includes setting aside notions of wrong and right, instead creating space to learn, connect, and lean into God.

When by sin, confusion, or pain we step away from one another, Christ guides us to reconciliation. We all are aware of stories where this doesn't happen. But here's the kicker, the story doesn't end in these temporal bodies or on this side of eternity. Our spirit lives forever and even if the reconciliation doesn't come in the present, it will come in the eternal future. There will be no dissension, separation, or distance in the full-fledged Kingdom of God. Until that day, Holy Spirit empowers us toward unity, love, and fullness.

Leverage Our Gifts for Abundance

God's master plan involves releasing power through His children. When we work in tandem, supporting and encouraging one another, our yield exponentially increases and we get to see the explosion of Jesus in our lives and the world around us.

> *"How good and pleasant it is when God's people live together in unity! It is like precious oil poured on the head, running down on the beard, running down on Aaron's beard, down on the collar of his robe. It is as if the dew of Hermon were falling on Mount Zion. For there the LORD bestows his blessing, even life forevermore." (Psalm 133:1-3)*

This is an overwhelming picture of God's presence and fullness springing through His people.

Too often the enemy gets the children of God to compare their gifts with each other. Succumbing to this ploy, we evaluate who is stronger or squabble over things we don't understand, fighting to be right and attempting to prove ourselves righteous. Our righteousness is a gift from God, a result of Jesus' efforts for us, not by anything we can earn. The Father also gives spiritual gifts, which are not earned. We are like children who have had training wheels removed from our bikes. We may bumble and struggle with our gifts at first, making mistakes, and accidentally running over someone's foot. Then with time, practice, and the training of Holy Spirit, we can utilize our gifts powerfully for the flourishing of the Bride.

Proverbs 31 is a beautiful picture of the Bride of Christ, the one Jesus is coming back for. She is awesome, powerful, and described as a military conqueror. She faces challenges, provides for the needy, and loves well,

"Who could ever find a wife like this one—she is a woman of strength and mighty valor! She's full of wealth and wisdom. The price paid for her was greater than many jewels. Her husband has entrusted his heart to her, for she brings him the rich spoils of victory. All throughout her life she brings him what is good and not evil." (Proverbs 31:10-12 TPT)

God desires His Bride to live out this incredible purpose. God is refining us to be a perfect Bride for Jesus.

God's heart for the flourishing of all His children is something that is increasingly realized in our unity. So let us reject the lies of the enemy. Let us identify and cultivate our talents, gifts, and the lane God has called us to ride in while encouraging our brothers and sisters in their gifts and lanes. As we do so we will break enemy lines, honor King Jesus, and bring joy to the Father.

Jesus loves us. We are His delight! He pursues His Bride with intense passion. Working through our differences, honoring each part, and cultivating our gifts unleashes power in the Bride to impact our world. Our unity shifts atmospheres, homes, neighborhoods, regions, nations, and the world. We carry the hope of glory. "To them God has chosen to make known among the Gentiles the glorious riches of this mystery, which is Christ in you, the hope of glory." (Colossians 1:27). We are the vessels of this living hope, impacting the world, preparing it for the return of the King.

CHAPTER 22

Cultivate Your Best to Give it Away

Cultivating one's best reminds me of the birthday celebrations in my wife's family. We have delicious outdoor potlucks from May to October, thanks to a number of birthdays and lovely Portland weather. It is a glimpse of Heaven! The one with the birthday picks the culinary theme, we've made Mediterranean, Mexican, and Indian feasts. Each family contributes a homemade dish, then we sit in the sun, eat, laugh, and play as kids, adults, and the occasional dog joins in the lovely revelry. These homemade dishes add depth, showcasing the skills and interests of the maker, and bring joy. Whether homemade ice cream, burgers, bread, salad, or pies, we "Taste and see that the LORD is good. Oh, the joys of those who take refuge in him." (Psalm 34:8 NLT).

This is exactly what God has in mind for his Bride, He wants us to bring our well-invested talents to the table as we gather in unity watching Holy Spirit pour His delight on the gathering. We honor God with our talents and He ignites the beautiful unity of our gathering. God loves excellence that is fueled by the love of doing something well. He created us to pour out the uniqueness of our identity. This may come through a home remodel project, one's ability to organize, or even how we relate to those we live with. God made us to enrich our environments. We are wired to release the goodness of God into the world for God's glory.

When we bring our best, we transform our environment. We are simply releasing the truth of Heaven that is living in us. We cannot change anybody, but our example and stance may cause somebody to encounter God and result in improvement in their life. This change can have a domino effect changing the culture, environment, and people around us, releasing fullness and causing good to flourish.

God wants to influence and is influencing every atmosphere.

> *"Jesus stood and cried out, saying, 'If anyone thirsts, let him come to Me and drink. He who believes in Me, as the Scripture has said, out of his heart will flow rivers of living water.' But this He spoke concerning the Spirit, whom those believing in Him would receive." (John 7:37-39 NKJV)*

The rivers that flow from Jesus to us and then through us are the influencing power that shifts atmospheres, changing people, families, even nations. As we drink of Jesus, Holy Spirit partners with us pouring into and through us. God desires to overwhelm the world with His transforming love.

Like torrential rivers cascading down a mountain when snow melts, God's will confronts, shakes, and even erodes environments. Making God's will known can feel opposed to maintaining space for freedom and choice. Yet God wants all to be saved,

> *"'I have come into the world as a light, so that no one who believes in me should stay in darkness. If anyone hears my words but does not keep them, I do not judge that person. For I did not come to judge the world, but to save the world. There is a judge for the one who rejects me and does not accept my words; the very words I have spoken will condemn them at the last day.'" (John 12:46-48)*

Healthy confrontation brings good and necessary tension. Truth not only forces a decision, it reveals God's character: that honors freedom, values choice, and shows that God has a will which He is implementing. He is the King of the Universe who provides salvation to all of His created beings who freely choose a relationship with Him. He has called us to be salt and light, holding space for and pursuing with grace those actively choosing sin. Simultaneously we live out Jesus' mandate, making disciples through sharing the gospel, training nations in the ways of God, and living righteously. To bring our best we must turn from evil, which seeks to steal our best. Next we learn to hold tension, develop our gifts, and apply our talents in excellence.

Jesus doesn't mince words about the severity and intensity of following Him. We have to rid ourselves of the things that lead to sin, steal our best, and distract our focus from Jesus.

> *If your hand causes you to sin, cut it off. It is better for you to enter life maimed than with two hands to go into hell, where the fire never goes out. And if your foot causes you to sin, cut it off. It is better*

*for you to enter life crippled than to have two feet
and be thrown into hell. And if your eye causes
you to sin, pluck it out. It is better for you to enter
the kingdom of God with one eye than to have two
eyes and be thrown into hell, where their worm
does not die, and the fire is not quenched. Everyone
will be salted with fire. Salt is good, but if it loses
its saltiness, how can you make it salty again?
Have salt in yourselves, and be at peace with each
other. (Mark 9:43-50).*

We cannot give our best if we are keeping a place
open for temptation and sin. To attain our best demands
the ruthless ridding of all that would induce compromise.

God wants us to be salty, to add flavor and preserve
what is good and holy in every environment He puts us
in. I believe salt and light expressed in God's people looks
like honing our best, promoting a culture of honor, and
encouraging the gifts God has placed in us. Simultaneously,
we need to be diligent to rid ourselves of everything that
attempts to steal the full vision of God from within. We raise
the bar, through honing and applying our talents, focusing
our efforts on the pure pursuit of Jesus, and crucifying the
sin that wants to entangle. The Bible exhorts,

*"Therefore, since we are surrounded by such a great
cloud of witnesses, let us throw off everything that
hinders and the sin that so easily entangles. And let
us run with perseverance the race marked out for us,
fixing our eyes on Jesus, the pioneer and perfecter
of faith." (Hebrews 12:1-2)*

Jesus set the pace, modeled how to run our race, and
now we are empowered by Holy Spirit to keep that pace.
When we respond to His call, run His pace, and raise the
bar, God causes a beautiful harvest to spring forth.

In It Together

We are one in Christ, and all that we do has a collective impact on the Bride. "God has put all things under the authority of Christ and has made him head over all things for the benefit of the church. And the church is his body; it is made full and complete by Christ, who fills all things everywhere with himself." (Ephesians 1:22-23 NLT). Through bringing our best we become a benefit to the whole, raising the bar for the flourishing of this interconnected unit.

Jesus shifts the focus of His followers from self-interest to desiring the health and flourishing of the entire community of God. God always works to bring His glory and redemptive purpose for the world through His people. Right before Israel took possession of the Promised Land, God emphasized to His people their choice of death or life.

"See, I set before you today life and prosperity,
death and destruction. For I command you today
to love the Lord your God, to walk in his ways,

*and to keep his commands, decrees and laws; then
you will live and increase, and the Lord your
God will bless you in the land you are entering to
possess. But if your heart turns away and you are
not obedient, and if you are drawn away to bow
down to other gods and worship them, I declare to
you this day that you will certainly be destroyed.
You will not live long in the land you are crossing
over the Jordan to enter and possess. This day I
call heaven and earth as witnesses against you
that I have set before you life and death, blessings
and curses. Now choose life, so that you and your
children may live and that you may love the Lord
your God, listen to his voice, and hold fast to him.
For the Lord is your life, and he will give you
many years in the land he swore to give to your
fathers, Abraham, Isaac, and Jacob." (Deuteronomy
30:15-20)*

This passage provides two keys for fullness. First, God didn't offer the Promised Land to the independent parts of Israel, rather to the nation as one. Though God blesses individuals for their choices, God characteristically honors the collective, united, choices of a people. We don't get to divorce ourselves from Christians who are doing things we dislike or disagree with. We may need to distance or remove ourselves from those holding unhealthy perspectives, however, we continue to intercede for the Bride's alignment to Jesus. Second, our choices have societal and generational impact, especially those in our family lines. We pass on positive or negative ramifications to people we will not meet this side of eternity.

God desires life for His people. From Adam and Eve

in the garden, to Israel in the Promised Land, to His Bride now and in the future. God gives freedom and choice, and God clearly lays out the consequences of what we choose. Furthermore, He so loves us that Jesus willingly took the curses that we chose, as His own, in order to create a redemptive path so that we could be together forever. God has already provided everything needed so that we can freely enter into His Kingdom.

Bringing our best means releasing the fullness of God through our lives for ourselves, our community, and our society. This includes the next generations. God wants us to experience His goodness in abundance. Jesus describes Himself as the good shepherd who cares for His sheep by protecting them and leading them to life. "I have come that they may have life, and have it to the full." (John 10:10b). He contrasts a good shepherd's desire to sacrifice and invest for the wellbeing and prospering of the flock, whereas a thief breaks into the pen to steal and harm the sheep.

In the presence of God, nothing broken, evil, or corrupt can exist. Yet many have become so used to living in brokenness and feel resigned to accept greater levels of pain and suffering than Jesus wants. In order to attain something, first you have to envision it. In Luke 6:45, Jesus highlights that what is in our hearts comes out of our mouths, "A good man brings good things out of the good stored up in his heart, and an evil man brings evil things out of the evil stored up in his heart. For the mouth speaks what the heart is full of." If we fill our hearts and minds with expectations and visions of brokenness, pain, and suffering, we will speak, expect, and receive these. But we can envision a victorious life which does not deny that pain and suffering but seeks to transform our experience of life through Jesus' inbreaking Kingdom. Many Christians are resigned to suffer through the worst until Jesus returns or they pass into glory. I believe a viable alternative is seeing ourselves as agents of Christ's victory who enforce the ramifications of His victory now.

Jesus encourages us in the hope of His victory. "I have told you these things, so that in me you may have peace. In this world you will have trouble. But take heart! I have overcome the world." (John 16:33). He also gives us eternal hope to latch onto.

> "Do not let your hearts be troubled. You believe
> in God; believe also in me. My Father's house has
> many rooms; if that were not so, would I have told
> you that I am going there to prepare a place for
> you? And if I go and prepare a place for you, I will
> come back and take you to be with me that you
> also may be where I am" (John 14:1-3)

Jesus takes our gaze higher than temporal suffering but to the place of forever bliss, this gives ample motivation to endure.

> "But God, being rich in mercy, because of the
> great love with which he loved us, even when we
> were dead in our trespasses, made us alive together
> with Christ—by grace you have been saved—and
> raised us up with him and seated us with him in
> the heavenly places in Christ Jesus, so that in the
> coming ages he might show the immeasurable riches
> of his grace in kindness toward us in Christ Jesus."
> (Ephesians 2:4-7)

Since we are seated with Christ in heavenly places currently, we have access to the first fruits of the fullness of eternity now. These passages don't hide the trouble we'll face; instead we're exhorted to fix our gaze on the hope, beauty, and power of a victorious eternity. This became real the moment we accepted the proposal of our saving Bridegroom.

Aligning with God unleashes elements of fullness now, allowing the Father's will to come through our lives. We all benefit by bringing our best, honing our skills, and fixing our gaze on the victory which overcomes the broken present for a future reality that is not far off. In the meantime, "Be devoted to one another in love. Honor one another above yourselves." (Romans 12:10). Through a lifestyle marked by caring, serving, and loving the Bride, we empower her.

Even a small percentage of Christians marked by this lifestyle can have a profound impact. Imagine how that would transform the world! A world where we relish life as it flourishes, where love and provision reign, and where we see the beauty of God.

In order to flourish, we have to break out of the scarcity, dog-eat-dog mindset that provokes us to rise above others through aggressively clawing over them. This destructive, win at any cost attitude, forgoes humility and breaks relationships. God designed us with skills that require our interdependence. Through partnering our talents with God and others, we flourish. We need to grow in our best, encourage the best in each other, and fix our gaze on living out the victory of Jesus.

Weakness is not a barrier for God.

> *"'My grace is sufficient for you, for my power is made perfect in weakness.' Therefore I will boast all the more gladly about my weaknesses, so that*

Christ's power may rest on me. That is why, for Christ's sake, I delight in weaknesses, in insults, in hardships, in persecutions, in difficulties. For when I am weak, then I am strong." (2 Corinthians 12:9-10)

Jesus will glorify Himself through our weaknesses and wants to flourish in our strengths. This requires acknowledging our gifts and honing them through a process of maturity so they will be of greater benefit. The Father delights as His children engage in His purposes to redeem and bring Him glory. God will not be stopped by our weakness, frailty, or initial incomprehension of what or how He is doing something. Yielding, co-laboring, and trusting Him allow His greatness to flow through us.

God gave each person unique and beautiful gifts which He wants to flow through for the benefit of the whole. We see prophets, pastors, teachers, and healers around the globe. In addition there are unique gifts all around us, gifts that make each of us who we are. Perhaps it's the ability to host, fix cars, build or repair homes, or a love for children and their development. It could be the ability to design a warm and inviting space, create a delicious meal, organize a room, or deal with legal documents. The point is, these gifts are blessings but not simply for us. They are also for our families, friends, and more broadly for the Bride. She exists to bless God and be a blessing to those she encounters.

When our gifts are operating on all cylinders, we build connection, prop others up, and provide ways for the love of God to pour through us and into the lives of others. The synergy of the gifts of the Bride bless even those who do not follow Jesus. God created each person to know and be overwhelmed by His love. When we support a nonbeliever, calling out his gifts, he experiences the love of Jesus, the very essence of what God created him for. God pours out gifts in order to bless us, others, and the world, so that He would be made known. The gift of Jesus' birth as prophesied in Isaiah 12:4-5, culminates with this charge for Israel,

> *"In that day you will say: 'Give praise to the LORD, proclaim his name; make known among the nations what he has done, and proclaim that his name is exalted. Sing to the LORD, for he has done glorious things; let this be known to all the world.'"*

God wants His glory known among the nations. He receives glory when we are aligned and this releases His blessings. All of eternity will be a love fest of blessing and beauty, enjoying God. No more begrudging days or tasks. We'll be caught up in the goodness and glory of God, drinking in more and more! The blessings and love we share now are tastes of the fullness of God's coming reign. We have more to look forward to!

CHAPTER 24

Firm Foundation for Future Generations

When my wife and I were Peace Corps volunteers in Ukraine, we served in a town with multiple volunteers. This proximity to others was highly abnormal for Peace Corps. Our transition from the United States to Ukraine had been stressful. Eastern Europe suffers generational wounds of distrust and betrayal, making it difficult to develop friendships. Having Peace Corps volunteers in our town provided a lifeline, encouraging us, and infusing joy. God wants to infuse us with hope and joy as we face the challenges of living in a war zone.

We were born behind enemy lines. At times we experience the harrowing realities of our sin-sick world under the influence of our enemy. We were not created to face the darkness alone. The alignment of the Bride supplies God's intended reinforcement of strength, unity, and power flowing through connection. "And let us consider how we may spur one another on toward love and good deeds, not giving up meeting together, as some are in the habit of doing, but encouraging one another—and all the more as you see the Day approaching." (Hebrews 10:24-25). Unity restores, empowers, and supplies vision to overcome the stresses of brokenness to obtain beauty and life to the full. Unity is especially important as trials intensify and the return of King Jesus draws nearer. The unity of Christ's Bride is not a nice suggestion, it is necessary, a prophesied reality that must occur. Perhaps we will face trials which will result in abdicating our independence. Trials can nudge or sometimes sharply prod us toward interdependence. Though harsh times are imminent, the beauty of a united Bride will outshine the darkness. This is already true of the persecuted church in places where the gospel is openly opposed.

In Ukraine, the community we had with other Peace Corps volunteers provided us with jolts of encouragement we needed to endure the challenges. Sometimes we'd bump into a volunteer while walking through town, quickly offload some stress, laugh about cultural challenges, and leave with our spirits lifted. We gathered to share meals, reflect on our journey with gratitude, and collaborated on details necessary for travel both for our work and vacations. Our times together refreshed our resolve to complete our service.

There is a parallel picture here of following Christ, Ambassadors of Heaven, foreigners living in the realm of a broken and dark world. When we gather with other believers to connect, encourage, pray, and worship, we receive a reality of the Kingdom of God coming. Hope, joy, laughter, promise, and vision mark the Kingdom.

Unity synergizes our corporate expression.

Jesus will return for His Bride, and she needs the support of all parts working together to realize the fullness of her beauty and power.

We need each other. It can be a challenge to admit this. We need to spur one another on with courage to run our race. God designed certain beauty to come by submission to each other. Relationship is the context for the power and movement of Holy Spirit. God's triune nature exudes beauty from connection. Our relationship with God comes with beautiful mysteries that don't fit in boxes of our control.

We have limitations and need each other to fill in the gaps in order to accomplish all that God wants. Though these can be frustrating at times, God beautifully uses our limitations.

Through linking our gifts, supporting one another, and being sources of encouragement, we flourish. Humbly embracing our limits and seeking help needed from one another is the path to strength. Put on the full armor of Christ (Ephesians 6:10-18), and use the weapons for our self defense, attack, and intervening to defend other members of the Bride. The list does not provide any protection for our backs. Our backs are protected through interdependence. This comes through prayer, fasting, calling out the good, admonishing the bad, and highlighting areas where we need to repent. The Bride must stand firm in unity, caring, contending, and advancing as one. This is not only for the people you understand and like, but also for those who are awkward, challenging, and difficult. Again we advance as a unit. If we do not advance together, we do not advance.

I believe we are in a unique time of history, much like what we read of the early church in the book of Acts, where God is highlighting unity and interdependence. As an American, I live from the context of a country that both celebrates unity, which birthed this nation, but also recoils at collective efforts due to a fiercely independent mindset. I recognize that Christians in some countries and contexts are living in greater unity. Some because their ethnic and national cultures value interconnected ways. Some because trial and tribulation force living in community to survive. I believe the Lord is leading His Bride to greater interdependence for survival and flourishing. I see it as a two-part call. On one hand, God is guiding us to be interdependent for the purpose of surviving trials. On the other hand, by honoring our different gifts and supporting one another in these, we will flourish in ways we have not yet experienced.

We will sink or swim based on the degree of unity we live out. I believe we are coming into days where we can no longer live our tunnel vision lives doing as we wish. Instead, we must learn to listen collectively and see how God is going to bring something more beautiful by our interconnected efforts. We have a free invitation to step into what God is doing, but it requires our active partnership; it will not simply happen. We have work to do, we have choices to make, and as always, God offers us life and death and He pleads with us to choose life. The next generation will reap the consequences of what we choose.

We have the opportunity to create a springboard of power through the degree of unity that we cultivate. It is the goal of good parents to leave abundance for their children and grandchildren. "A good person leaves an inheritance for their children's children, but a sinner's wealth is stored up for the righteous." (Proverbs 13:22). God is looking for His Bride to leave a good inheritance, including financial but also spiritual depth, values, and wisdom for future generations. May we be a generation that grabs the vision of God, and enters into the abundant fullness of God as we choose life. May it be said of us that we created an incredible foundation from which future generations built exponentially.

CHAPTER 25

United for Israel

In the independently minded West, one can easily disconnect from the communal, multigenerational story of God. God chose a people, Israel, to receive His covenantal blessing and desired them to be a conduit of His truth and blessing to all the people of the world. "Now if you obey me fully and keep my covenant, then out of all nations you will be my treasured possession. Although the whole earth is mine, you will be for me a kingdom of priests and a holy nation." (Exodus 19:5-6]. Many Christians have little connection to the Jewish people, let alone recognize that the Messiah is the Jewish man Jesus or Yeshua as He is called in Hebrew.

This is especially true for many Americans who have lost their ethnic roots, no longer tracing their heritages, and have not honored their unique immigrant story. Instead, indifference or shame slips in and results in people who have very little anchor to where they come from.

Disconnection from hereditary lines leads to abdicating

gifts and values received from previous generations and failing to champion these for future generations. This same attitude applied to a spiritual heritage results in a shallow expression of faith that misses God's desire to compound impact through the generations. This shortsighted perspective lacks the revelation that many of the things we work for now will not be fully realized until we cross into eternity.

Grasping as much of our family heritage history and spiritual legacy as possible will help us see ourselves as fulfillments of God's promise to Abraham. When we understand that, we develop a natural desire to honor the people who laid the foundation for our faith. Gentile Christians cannot separate out our Judeo roots. We are grafted into the beautiful tapestry of our Jewish ancestors. To turn our backs on Israel, dare I say, is anti-semitic. History validates time and again that those who oppose the Jewish people, end up on the wrong side of God's story. As the great Bible teacher Derek Prince frequently pointed out, Jesus chose to be a Jew for all of eternity.

In June of 2023, I had the incredible opportunity to travel to Israel with my sister on a tour that included six times of worship with worship leaders from Bethel Music. As cliche as it sounds, this trip changed my life. Being in Israel, at the Sea of Galilee, on the Mount of Olives, in Jerusalem, on Mt Carmel and visiting other holy sites shifted something in me. I have always held a conviction that supporting Israel is good and right, but in the past three years this conviction grew and I even yearned to travel to Israel. I gained new layers of depth of the story of God from this trip. I encourage every follower of Jesus to ask Him to take you to the Holy Land. My time in

Israel overwhelmingly affirmed that all Christians need to support the Jewish people, the nation of Israel, and God's redemptive story that is playing out with the Jews and the land.

I am diving into a tense and delicate topic in this chapter. But I believe healthy examination leads to a better understanding of the beauty of the Jewish people and the necessity of supporting Israel. Though I'm not a biblical scholar, I am a lover of God and have the faith of a child. God reveals His secrets to His lovers and those who meet Him with the faith of a child. I'm open to disagreement and correction so long as it is immersed in the grace and love of God. Let's stand with Israel, support the Jewish people, and long for our Jewish King Yeshua to return, echoing Revelation 22:20, "Come, Lord Jesus."

God loves the church and Israel. The Apostle Paul speaks to the complexity and beauty of the redemption of God that is both for Israel and the Gentiles in Romans 9-11. Paul highlights the Old Covenant with great honor, describing its beauty. He values it as the birthright of the firstborn,

> *"the people of Israel. Theirs is the adoption to sonship; theirs the divine glory, the covenants, the receiving of the law, the temple worship and the promises. Theirs are the patriarchs, and from them is traced the human ancestry of the Messiah, who is God over all, forever praised! Amen." (Romans 9:4-5)*

The church has not replaced Israel, rather the Gentiles have become blood washed children, entering into the New and Old Covenant promises of God by faith. Paul writes,

> *"the Gentiles, who did not pursue righteousness,*
> *have obtained it, a righteousness that is by faith;*
> *but the people of Israel, who pursued the law as the*
> *way of righteousness, have not attained their goal.*
> *Why not? Because they pursued it not by faith but*
> *as if it were by works." (Romans 9:30-32)*

The Old Covenant, beautiful as it is, could not bring people permanently into a right relationship with God. The Old Covenant was contingent on perfection, Jesus is the only human being able to fulfill the conditions through His sinless life and perfect sacrifice. His resurrection provides life to all, who by faith, obtain it.

God will fulfill His Old Covenant promises to Israel and by faith extends the promises of the Old and New Covenant to all who believe. Jesus' blood breaks all divisions and unites His Bride, all who receive the life of Yeshua, the true vine. The result is a cultivated olive tree, the Jewish people fused with the grafted in wild branches, the Gentiles.

> *"After all, if you were cut out of an olive tree that*
> *is wild by nature, and contrary to nature were*
> *grafted into a cultivated olive tree, how much more*
> *readily will these, the natural branches, be grafted*
> *into their own olive tree! I do not want you to be*
> *ignorant of this mystery, brothers and sisters, so that*
> *you may not be conceited: Israel has experienced*
> *a hardening in part until the full number of the*
> *Gentiles has come in, and in this way all Israel will*
> *be saved. As it is written: 'The deliverer will come*
> *from Zion; he will turn godlessness away from*
> *Jacob.'"(Romans 11:24-26)*

God did not desire the Jews to reject the Messiah, but being a great opportunist, He used the rejection as a way for vast numbers of Gentiles to enter the redemptive story of God.

The story of Israel's redemption is not over. The Apostle Paul explains of the Jews,

> *"Again I ask: Did they stumble so as to fall beyond recovery? Not at all! Rather, because of their transgression, salvation has come to the Gentiles to make Israel envious. But if their transgression means riches for the world, and their loss means riches for the Gentiles, how much greater riches will their full inclusion bring! ... For if their rejection brought reconciliation to the world, what will their acceptance be but life from the dead?" (Romans 11:11-12, 15)*

God is leveraging Israel's rejection of Yeshua to bring even more people into His family, using the salvation of the Gentiles to stir jealousy in Israel that will cause the Jews to gain a relationship with the Messiah. As Jews and Gentiles place their faith in Yeshua, the Bride displays the united beauty of the cultivated and wild olive tree. God desires fullness from her inseparable fusion.

God has not given up on Israel, His promises to her have not ceased. Jesus fulfilled the requirements of the Old Covenant, creating a way to God. His fulfillment of the requirements did not nullify the promises of God enacted to benefit His people. In fact God never abolishes things that He means for our good, Paul emphasizes this in Romans 11:29, "for God's gifts and his call are irrevocable." The church gets to experience the goodness of God's Old Covenant promises through being grafted into the cultivated olive tree. God's promises to Israel began when He promised Abram, "I will make you into a great nation, and I will bless you; I will make your name great, and you will be a blessing. I will bless those who bless you, and whoever curses you I will curse; and all peoples on earth will be blessed through you." (Genesis 12:2-3).

This promise is active, as followers of the Jewish Messiah, Yeshua. It is vital to support the Jewish people and nation of Israel, especially through prayer and intercession. There is room for discussion, questions, and disagreement about political policies. We can express concern about governmental matters and acknowledge the complexity of the Jewish, Palestinian, and Arab conflict. But in the midst of the complexity, we need to align with God's promises for Israel. To resist these is to resist God. The Bride especially needs unity in God's vision of Israel flourishing. The prophetic foretelling and redemptive timeline of the Bible involves Jesus' return to the Mount of Olives in the physical territory of modern Israel. Both the Old and New Testament contain prophecies which strongly suggest a defined national state of Israel is essential to the events that will unfold before Yeshua's second coming.

Zechariah 14 begins with a bleak picture of all nations coming against Jerusalem, brutally describing in uncomfortable detail the horror of a war torn and captured city. In verse 3 and 4 the story changes,

> *"Then the LORD will go out and fight against those nations, as he fights on a day of battle. On that day his feet will stand on the Mount of Olives, east of Jerusalem, and the Mount of Olives will be split in two from east to west, forming a great valley, with half of the mountain moving north and half moving south."*

I see Jesus' second coming in this passage. Zechariah

then says, "It will be a unique day—a day known only to the LORD—with no distinction between day and night. When evening comes, there will be light." (Zechariah 14:7).

Jesus references this day, "But about that day or hour no one knows, not even the angels in heaven, nor the Son, but only the Father." (Mark 13:32).

When Jesus returns, peace and justice will come, Jerusalem will be restored. Those who fought against Jerusalem will receive just and terrible consequences.

> *"The LORD will be king over the whole earth. On that day there will be one LORD, and his name the only name.*
>
> *It will be inhabited; never again will it be destroyed. Jerusalem will be secure. This is the plague with which the LORD will strike all the nations that fought against Jerusalem: Their flesh will rot while they are still standing on their feet, their eyes will rot in their sockets, and their tongues will rot in their mouths." (Zechariah 14: 9, 11-12)*

Jesus reiterates this,

> *"When the Son of Man comes in his glory, and all the angels with him, he will sit on his glorious throne. All the nations will be gathered before him, and he will separate the people one from another as a shepherd separates the sheep from the goats. He will put the sheep on his right and the goats on his left." (Matthew 25:31-33)*

Jesus will separate the sheep nations, those who supported Israel, from the goat nations, those who did not support Israel.

Supporting Israel, the firstborn, chosen people of God, is our privilege. Israel and the Bride are inextricably connected, the cultivated olive tree and the grafted in wild olive. Christians are adopted into Israel's redemptive story, we must champion her flourishing and unite for Israel.

Conclusion

Together we have a tremendous call. It involves grace, mercy, and a willingness to nurture depth of relationship. We have to learn how to support and cheer for all parts of God's body in the myriad of ways that God works through us. We must stoke the fires of hope, cultivate love, and learn how to honor each other.

Those who ran before us, passed the baton and we must run the race with every fiber of our being. We take back the territory that Jesus already owns and fight the lying foes, attempting to usurp the truth of Yeshua's reign and victory. We have a beautiful and challenging adventure, we are dependent on Holy Spirit for the breakthroughs to live out the flourishing vision of God. He wants to make us into lovers of Him and those who deeply love one another.

We have to have hard conversations. We have to grow and face the pain that comes through the process. It will sometimes be messy including failing, requiring us to admit our errors and sin. Yet via humility, an insatiable desire for God, and a willingness to lose everything for the beauty of His Kingdom, we will emanate Christ our King.

We are all searching for Jesus, whether we know it or not. We were designed for Him to yearn to spend the never-ending eternity basking in His love. The world is hungry for this revelation. We are the privileged messengers, tasked to reveal the Savior to the world He loves. Through our unity, the Bride testifies of this glorious and awesome truth.

We are going to make mistakes along the way, but that's not the end of the story.

Through pain we will learn, gain strength, and be transformed into the likeness of Jesus. "May the God who gives endurance and encouragement give you a spirit of unity among yourselves as you follow Christ Jesus, so that with one heart and mouth you may glorify the God and Father of our Lord Jesus Christ." (Romans 15:5-6). May the unity of the Bride reveal the glory of God within, repelling darkness, drawing the lost, and glorifying King Jesus!

Appendix: Unity in a Nation

I believe the history of the United States becoming a nation is an example of partnership with God. Scholar and biblical teacher Derek Prince, contextualizes the audacious nature of America's founding in his book, *The Pilgrim Legacy*. He writes:

> *"Because of the history of the world, as nations have arisen and fallen amid endless wars and bloodshed, the founding of America was utterly unique. It had never happened before, and it has never happened since. Reaching the shores of an unknown wilderness, a small group of people planted seeds—not seeds of military might, wealth, or power, but seeds of faith and freedom. And those seeds took root and grew."*[1]

The Pilgrims paved the way for this nation through humble and sincere faith, complete dependence and devotion to the character and will of God.

Prince comments on journals of William Bradford, a leader of the Pilgrims, who clearly identified:

> *"The Pilgrims' overarching objective: to open up the North American continent for the spreading of 'the gospel of the kingdom of Christ.' I like that*

---

1 Derek Prince, The Pilgrim Legacy (New Kensington, PA: Whitaker House, 2021), 22. Used with permission. All rights reserved. www.whitakerhouse.com

Bradford didn't just say 'the gospel.' He said 'the gospel of the kingdom of Christ.' It is significant that Jesus Christ Himself used this terminology in Matthew 24:14: 'And this gospel of the kingdom will be preached in all the world as a witness to all the nations.' There is a certain difference between preaching the gospel, and preaching the gospel of the kingdom. The gospel of the kingdom is a gospel of power, authority, and supernatural attestations. Without question, this 'great hope' of William Bradford and the Pilgrims has been fulfilled to a significant degree. America has definitely been a stepping-stone in spreading the light of the gospel of the kingdom of God around the world."[2]

God sustained this nation that started with a covenant and purpose to spread the gospel.

A covenant is a binding promise between two or more parties. Though the deck seemed stacked against the development of the United States, God partnered with the willing faith and audacious risk of the Pilgrims' voyage to spread the gospel, exercise religious freedom, and faithfully follow God. This cost them dearly, many died via the voyage to America, and in their first year, disease, famine, and a harsh winter caused more to perish.

Later in the story of this nation, God sustained the roughly organized and outgunned army of local militia soldiers. They were pastors, farmers, and blacksmiths by trade. Against all odds, they took on and defeated the British military super power. God made a way for these willing vessels to become free.

---

2 Prince, The Pilgrim Legacy, 54.

The Pilgrims' purpose of spreading the message of the gospel, the salvation available to all, is absolutely at the core of Jesus' mission. "For God did not appoint us to suffer wrath but to receive salvation through our Lord Jesus Christ. He died for us so that, whether we are awake or asleep, we may live together with him." (1 Thessalonians 5:9-10). This is God's relationship with each of us.

The Pilgrims understood this. They lived a lifestyle of prayer and fasting, fervently seeking God for guidance for each step of their journey from England to America. Their covenant with God and focus on His eternal mission guided all they did. "One of the most vital truths we see operating in the lives of the Pilgrims is the principle of 'covenant'."[3] The current Western mindset has lost the value for and dishonors the serious nature of covenant. Marriage is the most common form of covenant in Western culture but marriages frequently end in divorce. Many enter this covenant with a caveat replacing "til death do us part" with "until this isn't favorable for me".

The Pilgrims held a sacred view of covenant, aligning with God's heart, "It is very significant that this concept was present in the Pilgrim mindset. Why? Because God operates on the basis of covenant. Every time He has done anything serious and permanent in human history, He has done it with a covenant."[4] The Pilgrims understood for something of eternal significance to happen God enacts a covenant. They lived with great humility. "The Pilgrims committed themselves completely to do whatever God would reveal to them from His Word, no matter what it might cost. It is significant to note that, in doing so, they did not claim

---

3 Prince, The Pilgrim Legacy, 51.
4 Prince, The Pilgrim Legacy, 52.

to know it all."[5] They believed that God sought partners to spread the message of salvation worldwide and they willingly paid an incredible price, leaving all they knew for this purpose.

God's involvement in the establishment and freedom of the United States does not justify the atrocities, slaughter, enslavement, and trafficking that took place and continues taking place. God is faithful to covenantal partnership. "If we are unfaithful, He remains faithful, for He cannot deny who He is." (2 Timothy 2:13 NLT). The legalistic, loveless, finger-pointing mindset highlights poor decisions and sins, invoking shame and judgmental condemnation. God, however, redeems brokenness, pours out healing, blessing, and rewrites shattered stories in order to bring beauty and glorify Himself. God loves pouring His immeasurable power through weak and willing vessels, who are humbly submitted to Him. The Pilgrims lived this way.

God gives His children the honorable assignment to intercede and contend on behalf of others. Holy Spirit compels us to become conduits of restoration for our family, tribes, and nations. We get to envision any situation from the hope of heaven, magnifying God's desire and ability to bring beauty from chaos. The arguments of many, who don't believe God has had a hand in the formation and flourishing of the United States, often arise from their fixation on the evils in her history. When they become encumbered by the sins, the result is their inability to forgive. These sins become their evidence to assert God's inability to partner with the United States due to a messy past. But God keeps and honors the covenants that He made, even when subsequent generations willingly depart

---

5 Prince, The Pilgrim Legacy, 52.

from them. And God uses ugly, broken, and messy stories to bring about His transformation and beauty.

The revered Apostle Paul wrote a vast swath of the New Testament. Prior to his encounter with Jesus, Paul lived an incredibly zealous life opposing Christians. As the Pharisee Saul, he approved and supported the killing of Stephen (Acts 7:58-8:1), intentionally led efforts to destroy the church (Acts 8:3), and received synagogue sanctioned documents empowering him to round up, imprison, and kill Christians (Acts 9:1-2). We rarely introduce the truth of Paul's life, letters, and teaching with the qualifying statement, "Be sure to remember that Paul used to be a terrible enemy of the church and approved of the murder of Christians". We don't drag Paul's skeletons from the closet in order to present an accurate and honest assessment of his character and life. The reason we don't do this is Paul, as anyone who accepts the free gift of salvation, became a new creation through the blood of Christ. To bring the past up in a way that nullifies Paul's contributions actually slaps Messiah in the face. Paul does not hide his past, but he doesn't let the evils God rescued him from remain weights that hinder him from running his most focused race.

Nations are made up of people, God loves people. Jesus made provision for all people to have a relationship with Him. It would be inconsistent to say God is redeeming individuals but has no redemptive plan or interest in nations. As if nations are too complex for God to use for His purposes and plans. "The earth is the LORD's, and everything in it, the world, and all who live in it" (Psalm 24:1). We can't abdicate our national identities from what God is doing in the world. While in Athens, Paul spoke before a council primarily composed of Gentile, non-Jewish people,

"The God who made the world and everything in it is the Lord of heaven and earth and does not live in temples built by human hands. And he is not served by human hands, as if he needed anything. Rather, he himself gives everyone life and breath and everything else. From one man he made all the nations, that they should inhabit the whole earth; and he marked out their appointed times in history and the boundaries of their lands.

God did this so that they would seek him and perhaps reach out for him and find him, though he is not far from any one of us." (Acts 17:24-27)

God created and provides life to everything. God assigns the times and boundaries of the nations. God desires that human beings inhabit the whole earth in order that all people would reach for God. God loves His creation. Like a chess master, God weaves seemingly independent moves together that culminate in His objective to redeem the world.

I recognize that the origin story of the United States stretches over decades, involving multiple groups with a variety of motivations. Yet God wove a variety of people together for His purposes. As Paul asserts, God is working through everything. Though He opposes evil choices and abuses, He goes to work bringing a redemptive story from the wreckage. God is like a skilled coach, able to assemble a team combining people with distinct functions and strengths. He does this across generations as well as within the current timeframes we live in. He wastes nothing.

I believe black and white, narrow-minded thinking leads us to reject and disapprove of the whole messy story because of the grievous parts. We easily throw out the good because of something terrible in one chapter. God's redemption is not stopped by sin, rebellion, or evil. God has a habit of calling things as He sees them, which often does not align with our understanding of a situation. We have to make room for this and submit our understanding to God's assessment.

Though the United States has her flaws, horrific historical events, intentionally calculated, and incredibly sinful actions. Nonetheless, God honors and emphasizes the covenant and faith of the Pilgrims, their sacrificial voyage to America, and their desire to spread the gospel to the world. To breeze over this is to miss the essence of the national identity of the United States. This downplays her purpose from inception, that continues now, and will continue to flourish in the future. This also ignores God's desire to do eternally significant things through us. "Now to him who is able to do immeasurably more than all we ask or imagine, according to his power that is at work within us" (Ephesians 3:20).

God leads us in righteousness and also provides ways for the rebellious to return to Him.

In the book of Hosea, God instructs the prophet Hosea to marry a prostitute knowing she will leave him and have affairs. Yet God guides Hosea to bring her back and keep her as a wife through these betrayals. This is a picture of the way Israel acts toward God. God faithfully woos her back to Him

> "I will heal their waywardness and love them
> freely, for my anger has turned away from them.
> Who is wise? Let them realize these things. Who is
> discerning? Let them understand. The ways of the
> LORD are right; the righteous walk in them, but

the rebellious stumble in them." (Hosea 14:4, 9)

God heals the wayward and keeps His heart turned toward them. The rebellious will stumble when they encounter the right ways of God. God willingly holds the tension, He wants rebels to be redeemed. God is at work redeeming the rebellious components of the United States' history, and God is also sustaining the beauty within her.

Derek Prince offers these reasons for the United States' success:

> *"Some have argued that America's power and greatness are due to her abundant natural resources, combined with the heroic efforts and sacrifices of her people. This line of reasoning suggests that all its success is the result of fortuitous circumstances. But the reason is much deeper than mere coincidence. From the very beginning, the bright light that has shone from this nation has been powered from one source: an underlying faith in the living God. From its earliest days, America has been the 'great experiment.' It began as a representative republic, a land ruled not by a monarchy, aristocracy, or tyranny but by the laws written down in her constitution. This declaration of principles remains a remarkable document, hewn by men of great wisdom who were guided by the truths of God's eternal Word."[6]*

Our imperfect histories, whether of a person, tribe, or nation are redeemed through dependence and alignment with God. In the fabric of the United States, is a trust in God allowing for greater measures of success and

---

6 Prince, The Pilgrim Legacy, 14.

prominence than can be obtained by human efforts alone. The core convictions and commitments from the Pilgrims, settlers, Founding Fathers, and beyond provided an avenue for God's blessing, favor, mercy, and grace for future generations who intentionally rebelled against God.

The death of Jesus is the game changer, settling the judgment of God and releasing the love and redemption to all who willingly receive it. Even when a person, people, or nation stray, God's initial response is not judgment. "The Lord is gracious and merciful, slow to anger and abounding in steadfast love" (Psalm 145:8 ESV). Part of His grace is allowing time for redemption which, at times, allows the perpetuation of evil. God sees the end from the beginning;

> "Remember the former things, those of long ago;
> I am God, and there is no other; I am God, and
> there is none like me. I make known the end from
> the beginning, from ancient times, what is still to
> come. I say, 'My purpose will stand, and I will do
> all that I please." (Isaiah 46:9-10)

He has redemptive reasons that sometimes allow the person committing a heinous crime to continue a little longer, though God does not will the evil behavior. God is the great economizer, God wastes nothing, and God redeems everything that can be redeemed.

Though countries, cultures, and peoples have complexity and mess, God is still looking for those who partner with His purposes and ways. Just as each human story is full of good, bad, and ugly moments, God willingly partners with us even though we may have some horrendous chapters. This principle is true of nations as well. God actively looks to pour blessing and abundance even as we stumble forward, attempting to live out the good and holy.

In Matthew 25, Jesus speaks of the culmination of when He will come into His glory, prophesying about the separation of nations which will take place. There will be sheep nations, those who served Him and partnered with spreading the gospel of God's Kingdom and rule, and there will be goat nations, those who did not partner with God in this way. Jesus explains,

> *"When the Son of Man comes in his glory, and all the angels with him, he will sit on his glorious throne. All the nations will be gathered before him, and he will separate the people one from another as a shepherd separates the sheep from the goats. He will put the sheep on his right and the goats on his left." (Matthew 25:31-33)*

The United States of America has been one of the greatest global exporters of the gospel from its inception. The freedom and religious liberty that the Pilgrims sought and the Founding Fathers wrote into the Constitution allows the United States to be a haven for Jesus' Bride, allowing the unhindered proclamation of the Gospel. From the beginning, God protects freedom and choice. In the garden of Eden, He unrestrictedly placed both the tree of life and the tree of the knowledge of good and evil (Genesis 2:9). God honors and blesses people, families, tribes and nations who purposefully or even unintentionally align with what God calls good. The United States' protection of freedom and liberty is unprecedented for any nation in the world. This is a core reason why she has been so blessed and able to advance the truth of the gospel.

The United States has her flaws and her exportation of the gospel doesn't mean it has been shared effectively, efficiently, or even lovingly. Mistakes have been made every step of the way in developing this great nation. But God brings fruit from the scattered seed, and cultivates life through the hands of broken people. He honors the sower and His word will not return void, as Isaiah 55:11 affirms, "so is my word that goes out from my mouth: It will not return to me empty, but will accomplish what I desire and achieve the purpose for which I sent it". Even in our postmodern culture, the United States is still pivotal in sending the gospel.

The freedom of religion protected by the First Amendment of the US Constitution allows for the flourishing of numerous Christian ministries, missionary organizations, biblical software, online teaching tools, schools of ministry, and, of course, churches. God was looking for a nation that would champion this cause. The United States in all of her brokenness, partnered with God resulting in King Jesus receiving glory and more souls. The United States is not a self-made nation, it is a God-blessed nation because of covenant, commitments, and values held by her citizens historically, currently, and through ones that will be made by future generations.

The Pilgrims laid roots for the destiny of America, subsequent generations have laid hold of and continued holding to the heartbeat of heaven.

> *"Clean and strong throughout the length of the pattern, we may distinguish one thread of divine purpose. This purpose was born out of the fellowship of the Pilgrims and their united prayer and fasting. In each succeeding generation, it has been sustained and continued by the faith, prayers, and fasting of like-minded believers. The full and*

final outworking of this purpose still lies ahead."[7]

God wants to redeem the world, to show His beauty, to reveal His strong, united Bride, and to fulfill Matthew 24:14 "And this gospel of the kingdom will be preached in all the world as a witness to all the nations, and then the end will come." Before the return of Jesus, the United States will fulfill a pivotal role in the gospel of the Kingdom being preached worldwide.

> *"For the final outworking of His purposes, God is thus bringing together various resources that are needed: the human resources of Spirit-filled young people and the material resources of wealth and technology. In both these respects, the United States has a unique contribution to make."*[8]

The United States is not the only nation that God is using for special purposes. Thanks to the freedom and beauty of prayer shaping our country, we are positioned with great liberty to step into His purposes, untethered by challenges that many other countries face.

> *"This special purpose of God for the United States was born out of the fellowship of the Pilgrims. The vision God gave them was for the restoration of the Church. To this they devoted themselves with labor and sacrifice, with prayer and fasting. Today, those who share the Pilgrims' vision can see its fulfillment approaching."*[9]

Though I'm patriotic, I value every country and I

---

7 Derek Prince, Shaping History Through Prayer and Fasting. (Derek Prince Ministries - International, 2019), 189. Used with permission. All rights reserved.
8 Prince, Shaping History Through Prayer and Fasting, 205.
9 Prince, Shaping History Through Prayer and Fasting, 205.

believe that God will use all countries for the restoration and unity of His Bride. The United States is a blessed country and God is going to leverage the blessing to glorify Jesus in this hour. Every nation has a unique destiny to fulfill in the beautiful tapestry of God's story.

> *"The nation that first placed men on the moon is uniquely qualified to place the messengers of the kingdom gospel in every nation on earth. By the combined offering of its resources – both human and material – for the worldwide proclamation of the kingdom gospel, the United States will complete the thread of divine destiny that has run through its history for four centuries."*[10]

I believe in Prince's prophetic assessment. I believe in the unity, beauty, and power that have come through the tensions of sacrifice, commitment, and faithfulness through generations of Americans. I believe our greatest days are ahead of us. May Jesus receive the full reward of His suffering.

> *"In a loud voice they were saying: 'Worthy is the Lamb, who was slain, to receive power and wealth and wisdom and strength and honor and glory and praise!' Then I heard every creature in heaven and on earth and under the earth and on the sea, and all that is in them, saying: 'To him who sits on the throne and to the Lamb be praise and honor and glory and power, for ever and ever!'"* (Revelation 5:11-13)

---

10 Prince, Shaping History Through Prayer and Fasting, 205.

To contact Bradley email:
powerthroughtension@gmail.com

To order additional copies scan the QR code:

Power Through Tension - The Beauty of Unity

Power Through Tension - The Beauty of Unity Study and Discussion Guide

www.ingramcontent.com/pod-product-compliance
Lightning Source LLC
Chambersburg PA
CBHW062158080426
42734CB00010B/1736